THE JOURNEY FROM POOR PROCRASTINATOR TO INVESTED MILLENNIAL

Jeremy Kho

Copyright © 2018 Jeremy Kho

TABLE OF CONTENTS

PREFACE

Jeremy is a Y-generation, born in the 1980s. He came from a Southeast Asian country. His family wasn't rich, barely a middle-income. The story should be dated back to his childhood days when his parents ran a small business: a little coffee shop. The shop didn't bring them much wealth, but they worked hard for a living, and taught Jeremy and his siblings a great lesson about the importance of saving.

In 1997, Jeremy was eleven years old. The Asian financial turmoil hit the world. As a result, His father's investments in friends' and relatives' business had sunk into debt due to insufficient funds and excessive borrowing. His father had no other choice but to rent out the shop. His father went from being an employer to an employee. Then they started to struggle for their lives.

Although experiencing such a big crisis, Jeremy parents still tried their best to give him the education he deserved. They are definitely the most important mentors of his life. They showed him the importance of education while giving him the lessons of a lifetime -- the importance of financial knowledge, and the dread of being deep in debt.

Despite having learned his lessons, he was not fundamentally ready for financial knowledge. His desire for money blinded him. In his college years, Jeremy first got to know the money game, and this close to stepping into the trap of the pyramid. Luckily, logic had prevailed at that time and brought him back from the edge of the cliff.

The world had witnessed so much, from the Asian financial turmoil in 1997 to the Internet Bubble in 2000, and the financial crisis between 2008 and 2011, but as a Y-Generation He never experienced a real crisis, only to hear the whistle of it.

In the year 2010 and 2011, as a newbie to this business world, everything seemed fine, but his personal financial crisis was beneath the surface, waiting to emerge.

Jeremy started speculating in the foreign exchange market in 2011, and made some good profit out of it. At that time, investment in precious metals was peak, and he joined the wave of "the gold rush". He always made a quick profit during the monthly US nonfarm payrolls week, in the belief that he had found a goose with golden eggs.

In April 2013, with the upturn of US economy, Bernanke, then the chairman of the Federal Reserve, hinted at a withdrawal from the third round of quantitative easing (QE3), which led to a slump in gold values. Due to his ignorance, he didn't stop, thus losing all he had during that week. This was the crisis he experienced.

The same year, another "mentor" came into his life: the book, The Intelligent Investor by Benjamin Graham. He learned about value-investing, just like a person waking from a dream, and he realized that everything would come back to basics.

GREED AND SPECULATION ARE SOME KIND OF PROCRASTINATION.

Being greedy and speculative, Jeremy had been procrastinating in building his own financial foundation. Anything comes from something, as do money and wealth. Without a good foundation, money and wealth will be far away. If you want wealth, you need to be a provider at the same time to provide value.

So, with this specific purpose, He was off on the road from poor procrastinator to Invested Millennial.

INTRODUCTION

You picked up this book from the self-help or motivational section of the bookshelf, or maybe you downloaded it. Perhaps because you thought it was going to speak to you? You were going to find the time to read it just after you cleaned up the house, fixed the leaky roof, did the laundry and bought the groceries. But none of that ever happened. You didn't clean up the house, and neither did you fix the leaky roof. You abandoned the laundry, and you didn't buy any groceries. Consequently, you didn't get to read the book's awesome content, and even right now, while glancing cursorily at this preface, you think of dropping the book. "No one reads the preface anymore," you said.

I understand. Trust me, I get it. You are sick, affected with an ailment that has plagued the human race for centuries. It has left you static in life. I know exactly what ails you. It's that insidious disease known as procrastination.

Now you are curious. You know all about procrastination. However, you are in the dark as to how exactly it is ruining your life. Let's start from the beginning, shall we?

The word "Procrastination" originates from the Latin word "Procrastinare." If you consider its prefix and suffix, "pro" and "crastinus" translates to "forward" and "till the next day" respectively. Interesting, isn't it? Let's dump the Latin lessons for a moment. Procrastination simply means the avoidance of seeing a task to its accomplishment. I bet you knew that already. Been there, done that, right?

If it is any consolation, know that you are not alone in this. According to a study conducted in 1992, fifty-two percent of the surveyed student reported that they needed help with procrastination. In fact, eighty to ninety-five percent of college students are estimated to be procrastinators. The upshot of the quoted data is that we are all dealing with procrastination one way or another.

What does this have to do with you? Hold on, we are getting there.

Now you might argue that your relationship with procrastination is due to your tendency to get everything right and that you can't help it. You might even argue further that you have the tendency to negatively evaluate outcomes and your own performance. In psychology, that argument would be considered a coping response to procrastination. It is called a delusional attribution to external factors. However, because this book is not really a psychology text, we'll just label your argument "hogwash." It's a way to justify that which is ruining your life.

We all procrastinate in different aspects of our life. This includes academics, social, health, spiritual, etc. But perhaps the most hazardous type is financial procrastination. Basically, it is the payment of your electricity bill two weeks after the due date. In case you are wondering if you are a financial procrastinator, don't bother. The subsequent chapters will take care of that.

"The best time to plant a tree was 20 years ago. The second best time is now.".

Chinese Proverb

Although you might have picked up this book from the self-help section, and I might have thrown in some inspiring quotes, heretofore, to boost your morale, believe me when I tell you that this is not a motivational book.

It wasn't written to motivate you all the way to financial freedom, nor was it created to get you off your butt into a long-term investment. No! It was written to tell you what will happen if you don't.

CHAPTER ONE

WHAT IS FINANCIAL PROCRASTINATION?

Paul Carter stared blankly into the darkness; his eyes could not make out anything in the room. However, his ears could. He could hear his neighbor's sound system blasting away in the dark. Instantly, he understood exactly what had happened. His power supply had been cut off again for not paying his bill. Paul wasn't poor, neither was he broke - at least not yet. He had the money to pay; he just had never been able to create the time to pay his bills. But you can't blame him, He never had to. Lisa, his ex-wife, used to handle the finances. Now Paul was running into financial problems. Although he had a good job that paid him quite well, his credit card balance was increasing with every new month. He pays his bills and fills his taxes at the very last minute, sometimes late. Perhaps what scared Paul the most was the fact that he was a 35-year-old man who has zero savings and no investment. He had always told himself he would start saving as soon as he was done with the student loan. That never happened. There was still a student loan to pay, and the bills were still pouring in. Paul Carter has a problem; he is a financial procrastinator.

Finally, you can ask the million-dollar question you have been dying to ask. What is financial procrastination? If procrastination is the action of delaying or postponing, and finance is the management of money and credit, then financial procrastination can be defined as the conscious decision to avoid or delay all matters relating to one's financial affairs.

The interesting thing about this definition in relation to Paul Carter's problem is that Paul actively and decisively made a decision to delay his financial matters. It is not a subconscious decision. It is a conscious one. It is also inevitable that with Paul it will be a recurring problem. But how did Paul become a financial procrastinator?

FINANCIAL PROCRASTINATION, WHY IT HAPPENS

1. Fear of The Financial Unknown

A large percentage of us avoid dealing with our financial problems because we are afraid of opening a Pandora's Box. We expect the worst about our financial status, and almost plunge ourselves into depression. We deal with this by repressing the worries in the basement of our deepest, darkest corner of our mind, never to be considered again. But guess what? It isn't that bad.

2. You Treat Your Financial Affairs Like It's Calculus

Before you start wondering about the relationship between your financial affairs and calculus, take a moment, dig deep into your mind, and think. The only reason we never understood calculus is because we assumed it was too difficult to be understood by mere mortals such as ourselves. Oddly enough, we still do. Now as grown-ups, we have subsumed our financial affair into the same category as calculus - the "simply too difficult to understand" category. If you cut through the whole storytelling, and uncover the real reason it has fallen into the STDTU category you'll find out that it all leads back to reason number one– fear of the financial unknown.

3. You Conjure Up Dragons to Slay Before Getting to Your Financial Affairs

Sometimes we place ourselves in the shoes (or armor) of a knight with our financial affairs sleeping right up there in the castle, and the dragon standing defiantly in between, determined to prevent us from reaching our goal. Firstly, let me start by saying that dragons do not exist, but your financial issues do. That said, people in this category usually choose some type of obstacle to overcome before dealing with their personal finances. It doesn't matter if the obstacles are real or imaginary; it still serves the same purpose, and that is to deter us from reaching our financial goals. In Paul Carter's case, the invincible dragon was his student loan.

Don't get it wrong. Some of the reasons behind the lag about financial affairs are valid and legitimate. However, the dragons exist as an excuse for not doing what needs to be done.

4. Fear of Looking Dumb

There is a deep fear common to all of us. The fear that prevented us from asking questions during History lessons about the Gettysburg address. The same fear that prevented us from being more than average in college. That is the fear of looking dumb. This reason is more universal than you think. People generally want to appear like they have control over their finances. So, rather than seek the service of a financial advisor, they file it away somewhere deep in the closet. When asked about it, they make statements like "I have it under control" or "It's been handled." You don't have it under control, financial affairs don't handle themselves! Get help now. Being dumb, in a bid to look smart, is such a dumb thing to do.

5. Our Financial Affairs Bring Out Our Inner Ostrich

This is an avoidant approach to problem solving. Like ostriches, we see our financial affairs as a predator to be avoided. We bury our heads in the sand and hope it will go away. People in this category avoid responsibilities; they deny obvious facts and refuse to accept advice. They naively hope that denying the existence of a problem will make it go away. When you finally get your head out of the sand, your financial affairs will still be standing right there, staring you in the face.

Now that you know why financial procrastination occurs, you may be wondering if you are a financial procrastinator. Here is how you will know.

- **Paying Bills and Filing Your Taxes:** A financial procrastinator would delay all matters relating to bill payment. You'll end up incurring additional payments in the form of late fees, which will

further plunge you into financial crisis over time. The same thing applies with filing your taxes. If you are sitting in the dark like Paul Carter because you haven't paid your electricity bill, you are a financial procrastinator.

- **You Have Zero Savings and No Investment:** Like Paul Carter, you have a job that pays you well. Like Paul Carter, you don't bother yourself with savings, neither do you think of investments. Maybe, unlike Paul Carter, you have no student loan to pay. However, like Paul Carter, you are definitely a financial procrastinator.

- **You Postpone Grocery Shopping:** Harmless as that sounds, it is a symptom of a greater crisis. When you repeatedly postpone grocery shopping, it hurts you financially, aside from the truth that it is also a form of procrastination. You spend a lot of on fast food and get too many groceries when you choose to buy, to overcompensate for never buying in the first place.

"You must gain control over your money or the lack of it will forever control you."

Dave Ramsay

Bottom Line: You already know what financial procrastination entails. You know exactly why it happens, and you know the signs that can help you determine if you are a financial procrastinator. It is not enough to ascertain your financial procrastinator status. You must be willing to change.

Chapter Two

Are You Being Reactive or Proactive in Finance?

Sam and James were brothers, who everyone considered shrewd. Sam was a truck driver in Dallas, and so was James. Sam didn't earn much but always did manage to save a little. He had mastered the art of delayed gratification. James earned just as much as Sam, but he wasn't interested in the art of saving. "Money was made to be spent" he would say.

While Sam spent his free time learning the basics of investment such as ownership investment, fixed-income investment, mutual fund investing, tax-deferred investment, among others, James bought beers for the guys at the bar during his free time. Accordingly, Sam's kid got into college on paid tuitions, and James's kid had to apply for a student loan.

A couple of years later, Sam bought the truck company he used to work for. He became a business owner. James still worked in the truck company, expecting weekly wages from Sam. Sam was smart; he had a lot of investments. James was not, he had a lot of debts. There was Sam, and then there was James. They were brothers, but only one was shrewd. Sam was an investor; James was a spender. Be like Sam, not like James.

In case you are wondering what it really means to be proactive and reactive in affairs of finance, look at Sam, and then look at James. Then ask yourself who the proactive brother was.

Let's start with the basics here as we consider the keyword here – **initiative.** A reactive person lacks initiative. He subjects his goals under the unstable whims of situations. He acts only in response to an event, never in preparation. Being reactive is not entirely a bad thing. As humans, the reaction is an integral part of our survival. Classic examples include the knee-jerk and our "fight or flight" reaction initiated by the activation of the sympathetic nervous system. Being reactive is our inner caveman's response to danger.

Armed with foresight, and the initiative to act on the knowledge derived from it, a proactive person gets ahead of situations. He is never caught unaware by the unbalanced state of affairs. He has possessed the grace to navigate through sticky situations by separating manageable threats from the non-manageable ones and produce the appropriate response. A proactive person has his mental world evolved from years of devoted learning. He never acts impulsively. Now that you know what it means to be proactive and reactive, let us approach it functionally in the world of finance.

BEING PROACTIVE OR REACTIVE IN FINANCE

In the world of finance, being proactive and reactive goes beyond initiative, it is about control. In your relationship with money, who calls the shots? Do you perceive money as a concept couched in a piece of paper meant to be used as a tool? Or you regard it as the all problem-solving deity. Do you spend based on what you earn, or do you earn based on what you spend?

It is not my intention to complicate matters so let me simplify it. As far as personal finance is concerned, procrastination can lead to reactive responses. This means that we do not handle our financial issues until it is too late. When we do not set deadlines for ourselves to incite some sort of proactive financial planning, we tend to do nothing. We accept the confidence-damning belief that our financial lives are happening to us. We allow ourselves to be tossed around by our financial lives, effectively relinquishing control to money.

In a reactive approach to finance, you are driven by your financial necessities and thus incapable of planning. Consequently, you make a lot of impulse purchases based on the "deal of the day," with total disregard for the consequences. You are absolutely dependent on what you earn; therefore, you find it difficult to make ends meet in times of financial emergency. Basically, the reactive approach is a caveman approach towards your financial needs as it is driven by survival. The goal is to stay alive till you receive the next paycheck.

As expected, proactive approach toward finance is the complete opposite of its reactive counterpart. Here is how to take a proactive approach towards financial issues you should know.

Plan Ahead

This is actually what it means to be proactive in finance. Planning ahead is all-encompassing. It includes anticipating and attending to your short-term financial goals (e.g., grocery shopping, utility bills, etc.), while not losing sight of the long-term ones (e.g., College tuition, buying a house). Start by setting priorities for your spending. You can plan for your short-term financial goals by budgeting. Apart from curbing impulse buying, budgeting also gives you the opportunity to attain your long-term goals through saving.

Emergency Savings

Another step towards being proactive about your finance is by creating emergency savings. These savings should be different from your normal savings. It is your safety net in case you incur some type of additional, unplanned expense. What's more, the presence of some money somewhere, which you could use in case of any crisis, ensures you sleep well at night.

High ROI Expenditure

Without a whit of doubt, seeking a high return on your investments is an important step to take towards your financial freedom. However, this can begin with seeking a high return from household expenditures such as swapping out 15 incandescent bulbs with more energy-efficient bulbs, like LEDs or CFLs. This simple action could save you $50 a year. According to the Department of Energy, adding insulation will pay for itself within a few years, thanks to cheaper heating bills. Not only is this good for the environment, but it can also save you a lot of money in the long run.

Manage Cashflow

It's time for you to start earning what you spend. Start by creating multiple sources of incomes. Don't get it wrong, this has nothing to do with savings, and everything to do with investments. Ownership investment, fixed-income investment, mutual fund investing, or tax-deferred investment, it doesn't matter. Just make sure you make an investment periodically. Next, manage your lifestyle to fit. This can start in the form of having a nice homemade dinner with your family, rather than eating out in an expensive restaurant. This will save you from all those credit card debts.

"I believe that everyone chooses how to approach life. If you're proactive, you focus on preparing. If you're reactive, you end up focusing on repairing."

John C. Maxwell

Bottom line: The first step you have to take towards curing yourself of financial procrastination is to become proactive. However, if you remain too lazy to get off your butt, and work towards your financial freedom, the consequences are dire.

CHAPTER THREE

THE COST OF FINANCIAL PROCRASTINATION

As said earlier, there are a couple of dire consequences associated with procrastination. These costs can range from, missed deadlines to wasted opportunities. Even though the cost of procrastination is quite significant, putting it in quantity, we can relate with is not as easy.

However, one type of procrastination we can easily quantify is that relating to our personal finances. Financial procrastination can be estimated in money lost, either through the incurred expense, or lost opportunities.

FIVE COSTS OF FINANCIAL PROCRASTINATION

These are the costs of making a conscious decision to avoid or delay, all matters relating to one's financial affairs.

1. Sloppy Organization of Personal Finances

The cost of financial procrastination always reflects first in your personal finances. However, during the distractions of our daily lives, we tend to underestimate the importance of organizing our personal finances.

The sloppiness in your personal finance that can cost you the most is credit card payment. This can hurt your finances in different ways. The obvious way is that you're penalized with a $25 fee first violation, subsequent violation within six months can attract as much as $35 in penalty.

That's not all if you don't get your act together, and end up missing two consecutive payments again, your credit card company can decide to increase your interest rate. The implication is that you will be required to cough up more money for any balance you carry from one billing cycle to the next.

What's more, the side effect of late payment never goes away. The impact will always reflect on your credit score. Those payments you never made, can eventually end up as a red flag on your credit report. Consequently, potential lenders will charge you a higher interest rate as you are a high-risk borrower, as reflected by your credit report. This can cost you thousands of dollars more, particularly in interest costs for big items such as a house or a car.

Another sign of sloppiness in the handling of your personal finance is the buying of the last-minute gift. The problem with this, according to Andrea Woroch, a consumer expert, is that people feel less price-conscious when they feel pressured to buy something quickly.

How do you fix this problem? Organize your personal finance by taking the following steps.

- Use automated payments to ensure that you pay your bills on time.
- Use the calendar app on your phone to remind yourself of upcoming bills due.
- Finally, order your goods online. You have a good chance of scoring better deals there.

2. Deferrals in Investment

In investment, timing is everything. Failure to make your investments when you are supposed to can be quite costly. Now, imagine a situation where you invest $2,000 every year from the age of 30, in a tax-deferred account, say an individual retirement account (IRA). With a long-term average annual rate of return of 5%, you'll end up with a total of $132,878. If you had made that exact investment at 40, at that same average annual rate of return, you would have just about half of that money.

Basically, every day you fail to open a retirement account, you lose good money. According to Bob Gavlak, a CFP® with Strategic Wealth Partners in Independence, Ohio, "Not only do you get a tax deduction, but in the case of a 401(k), you may get a match from your employer... [Your retirement account] is extremely valuable," he concluded.

3. You Cab Around the City

You reside in a big city, and you are always running late. Consequently, you pay some ridiculously humongous price in cab fare, when you could so easily have taken the much cheaper public transport. Let's do the math, shall we? A five-mile ride in a taxi costs $19.30 in New York City. However, that same distance in the same city will cost just $2.50 if you opt for the subway. In Boston, you'll have to pay $16.20 for a cab ride, and $2.10 for the train. The figures vary depending on the city, but the price difference is the same. Public transport is always cheaper. To know exactly how much your financial procrastination is costing you in cab fare, simply subtract the amount you pay for cabbing around from how much you would have had to pay, had you taken the train.

4. Late Filing of Taxes

We established in the previous chapter how financial procrastination is always directly proportional to the unpleasantness of the task that requires your financial attention. Based on this assessment, the filing of taxes is probably the most procrastinated financial affair, and April 15 is probably the most dreaded date for all financial procrastinators across the United States of America. In truth, it is prudent to file taxes when due. This is because, the interests you would be required to pay, can make late filing quite expensive for you. Let me explain how.

A minimum and maximum penalty of 5% and 25% respectively of the tax payable is charged by the IRS for the failure of filing income tax returns when due. Bearing this in mind, if for some vague, unknown reason, you are unable to meet the tax filing deadline. For those vague, unknown reasons, you ended up filing six months late. This is how much you would have to pay. Let's say your tax balance payable is $5,000, your "failure-to-file" penalty (minus interest) would be $1,250. Your financial procrastination would cost you a total of $1,250. That's a huge sum to pay for procrastination, don't you agree?

5. Procrastination as a Tool for Innovation

I get it, you are surprised. But as much as procrastination can serve as a barrier to your financial freedom, according to Adam Grant's (a professor of management at Wharton) interview with Business Insider, procrastination is a tool required by innovative thinkers. He went on to explain that procrastination is a vice when it comes to productivity, but a virtue as far as creativity is concerned.

"Habitual procrastinators will readily testify to all the lost opportunities, missed deadlines, failed relationships and even monetary losses incurred just because of one nasty habit of putting things off until it is often too late."

Stephen Richards

Bottom Line: There is no big speech here, the conclusion is glaring. Avoid financial procrastination, plain and simple. Unless you are some type of creative genius. In which case, procrastinate away. Maybe you'll be the next George R.R. Martins, and write a new Game of Thrones series for us to enjoy. Then again, you might also never finish the work.

CHAPTER FOUR

HOW TIME VALUE OF MONEY AFFECTS YOU

There was a man who had two sons. The younger one said to his father, 'Father, give me my share of the estate.' So, he divided his property between them. Not long after that, the younger son got together all he had, set off for a distant country and there squandered his wealth in wild living.

Luke 15:11NIV Bible

That's a quote from one of the most popular parables of the new testament in the Bible; the parable of "The Lost Son." I know you are wondering what it has to do with finance. Hold on, stick with me, and I won't disappoint.

First of all, I understand that the younger one demanding for his share of his father's estate was tantamount to wishing his father dead. But for a moment, forget what you know, think outside the box. Only then, can we create another version of this story together.

33

Now imagine that the name of the elder brother was Jake, and the younger one was Dean, and they were both sons of a millionaire. Let's call the father Bill.

Jake was reserved, he liked to play it safe, and he was no risk taker. Some would even say he lacked the guts. Dean, on the other hand, was a vivacious young man who was an adrenaline junky. So, it didn't surprise their father when his younger son Dean approached him to demand his half of the inheritance. Bill was neither angry nor worried, he simply called his accountant and arranged a whopping sum of $70 million for his son.

Dean collected the money, determined to make something great of himself, he moved out of his father's mansion. Now imagine for a moment, that the prodigal son didn't squander the money. He invested as much as he could and spent as little as he could. Five years later, their father died of lung cancer. He smoked too many Cubans. Jake finally got his own $70 million inheritance. The rest of the fortune was donated to charity. By then, his younger brother had made an additional $40 million. Dean was now worth $110 million. That's $40 million more than what Jake had. Moral of the lesson; money in hand is always a sure thing. This brings us to a concept that is considered a fundamental principle of finance. From everything related to purchasing and investing; time value of money. Starting from the most obvious question.

WHAT DOES THE TERM "TIME VALUE OF MONEY" MEAN?

Time value of money is a concept that explains how time affects monetary value. Specifically, how purchasing power differs with the passage of time. Simply put, a dollar today is much more valuable than a dollar in the future. Get ready now, we are about to delve deeper.

In our version of the prodigal son, the younger one collected his inheritance earlier because he understood this basic principle. The question is, what are the advantages and disadvantages of the decision made by Dean?

There are three basic reasons why the prodigal son was right in collecting the money.

- A dollar in hand is much more valuable than a dollar in the future. That dollar can be invested, can generate interest over time. That dollar in hand has potential earning power.

- Money is subject to inflation. It will reduce the purchasing power of the money. Hence, reducing the worth over time.

- Finally, there is that risk of not actually receiving that money in the future. Having that money in hand effectively eliminates that risk.

- These are different ways to comprehend how time value of money affects you:

HOW TIME VALUE OF MONEY AFFECTS YOUR PERSONAL LIFE

1. Professional Athlete Pay

As a professional athlete, you are entitled to a set amount of money for the season. However, depending on the sport you are into, you can lose your future earnings if you get injured, especially off the pitch, track, or court.

Based on your understanding of time value of money, a decision to get your cash upfront would always be in your favor. Rather than wait for some future payment that is not sure, you can collect your money in the form of a signing bonus.

2. That Pretty Black Dress

You fell in love with this black dress down at the store. So, you checked the tag, the price was just as steep as it was pretty. But you didn't care, you simply charged it on your credit card and danced all the way home. Six months later, you finally had the money to pay off your balance. To your dismay, you had to pay more for that pretty black dress you love so much. The time value of the money was being added in the form of credit card interest.

The best way to avoid paying for the time value of money as far as a credit card is concerned is for you to pay off the balance right away.

3. Your Big Lottery win

You won a hundred million dollars in lottery, that's awesome. Now you have a decision to make. Do you opt for 30 years of future annuity payment, or do you pick the immediate cash payout?

The answer is pretty easy. The fact that you will have immediate control of your money, which you'll be able to immediately invest is enough reason to opt for an immediate cash payout. Plus, you would be avoiding the risk that the lottery commission, for some reason, might end up not paying down the line.

How Time Value Of Money Affects Your Business.

It's not just your personal life that is at risk of being influenced by time money value, your business is as well. The effect of time value of money is felt more in your business because of the important role it plays in your profit. Here are ways it affects your business.

- **Capital Budgeting**

It is necessary to understand the effect of time value of money on your capital budgeting. This is because any project worth pursuing must have a return that will make up for what is costs. Such return must cover the upfront costs (which most project always require), and interest acquired through time value of money.

• Negotiating Contracts

Time value is quite important to businesses that negotiate contracts for payment. For example, ABC constructions offered the same service as XYZ constructions. However, ABC negotiated a contract that would require its client to pay $100,000 in one year, XYZ negotiated a contract of the same amount, but payment would be collected upfront. By choosing to collect their full payment, XYZ Constructions was able to make other investments, and worry less about if the client could afford their service. Most importantly, they got the true value of their money. The same cannot be said for ABC constructions that collected their money one year later.

This is why some companies offer discounts to clients that pay in advance for services rendered. They are trying to capture the time value of the money.

• Discount Rate

The most important factor when calculating the time value of money is the discount rate. This helps business owners with the translation of current value into future value and vice versa. Let's use ABC constructions as an example again. The company collected $100,000 full payment because they understood that with an annual return on investment of 5%, they would easily have $105,000 by the end of the year. Meanwhile, if they waited a whole year before collecting the payment, the money would be worth $95,000 in today's dollars.

Perhaps the best way to really understand how the time value of money affects us is by knowing how to calculate how much it costs us in dollars. The next chapter explores that.

"Money makes money. And the money that money makes, makes money"

Benjamin Franklin

Bottom Line: In our version of "The Prodigal Son," Dean understood the concept of time value of money. He understood the power of purchasing power of money at hand, and how to make it work for him. He was a proactive young man that acted deliberately to achieve his financial freedom. You cannot hate him for that, you can't hold a grudge against him. His father didn't.

CHAPTER FIVE

HOW MUCH DOES IT COST YOU?

We have talked about the time value of money; you already understand how it affects your personal life and business life. The question now is, how much does it cost you in dollars?

THE COST OF TIME VALUE OF MONEY

The calculation of Net present value is an easy way to answer this question. It is a calculation that compares the money you receive in the future with the amount received today, without forgetting the role of time and interest in the calculation.

To comprehend fully how much the time value of money costs you, you need to be able to account for specific variation in the calculations which are;

- Present Value: The current worth of future money, given a specified rate of return

- Future Value: Future value of the cash you have now.

There are five factors to consider when calculating the time value of your money. These are;

✓ A number of time period involved, usually measured in months, or years.

✓ Annual discount or interest rate.

✓ Present value.

✓ Payment

✓ Future value.

Allow meto introduce you to these two formulas that will enhance your perspective on time value of money.

How to Calculate Time Value of Money Using the Future Value of a Lump Sum

Future value of a lump sum is a time value of money formula used to calculate how much money you will have at a particular time based on your decision not to spend them. First of all, the formula.

FV = pmt (1+i) ^{N}

Where "FV" stands for Future Value, "Pmt" stands for Payment, "I" represents the Rate of return you expect to earn, and "N" equals Number of years.

Relax, it's not calculus. It's just a little calculation. Let's use our imagination too, paint a picture to help understand the application of this formula.

Now imagine that it was September. Why is September special, you ask? Well, that's because you had been waiting for that new Apple iPad. You had wanted it from the first moment you saw it on TV, and It was supposed to be available in Apple stores in the second week of September. So, you stayed up all night on a queue with the geeks and early adopters. However, before dawn, you began questioning if spending $400 on another iPad was really a good idea. Your options are known. You could either buy the latest Apple iPad or invest the money in your index fund, maybe your blue-chip portfolio. You could gift it to someone in 30 years. You needed to know the opportunity cost. So, you pulled out your calculator.

Before we input the figures, here are some things you should know. Large market capitalization stocks have returned 10%, while small market capitalization stocks have returned 12%. This is especially true when you buy using a low-cost, tax-efficient, buy-and-hold investing strategy. When you have very little to no turnover, you have a sound dividend reinvestment plan, and maintain dollar cost averaging to take advantage of market collapses.

With that knowledge, you chose to go with a more conservative figure. Rather than using 10% or 12%, you calculated a future compounding rate of 8%. So, you inserted the relevant figures in the formula.

FV = pmt (1+i) ^{N}

Where "Pmt" = $400, "I" = 8%, "N" = 30

Step 1 FV = $400 (1+.08) ^{30}

Step 2: FV = $400 (1.08) ^{30}

Step 3: FV = $400 (10.0627)

Step 4: FV = $4,025

Interesting, isn't it? I know what you are thinking. You think the figure is wrong, we didn't account for inflation. Surely, inflation plays an important role, the value of money cannot remain constant for twenty-five years. You know what, you are right. Inflation represents a loss of value; we must account for that loss.

Adjusting This for Inflation by Using the Present Value of a Lump Sum Time Value of Money Formula

This is where we introduce the second time value of money formula. It is called "Present Value of a Lump Sum." We can account for inflation using this formula by taking the future value (FV) from our previous calculation and discount it back to the present at an estimated inflation rate. Yes, it's that easy.

Let's imagine you estimated that inflation is going to run 3% over the next 30 years.

PV = FV / (1+i) ^{N}

Where PV = Present Value, FV = Future Value, Pmt = Payment, I = Discount Rate, N = Number of years

You already know the relevant figures, let's plug it in.

Step 1: $4,025 / (1+.03) ^{30}
Step 2: $4,025 / (1.03) ^{30}
Step 3: $4,025 / 2.43
Step 4: $1,656

By choosing not to spend $400, you would actually save $1,656. The question here is simple. Between buying a $400 iPad (which will definitely lose value over time), and having an extra $1,656 (in an equivalent of today's purchasing power) 30 years from now, which do you find more appealing? Now, you can argue that you will probably be richer thirty years from now. Truth is gifting it to other people (maybe your niece, or nephew for Christmas) can be just as rewarding. There is also a viable option of donating it to charity organizations.

Develop a habit of analyzing your spending. Do a quick calculation in your head every time you want to buy something you don't really need. How much would you be earning by not spending that money? Then, set up an account for any decision to forego spending. You can even call it DFS account. For every spending, you forego, put the money in the account. Let it work for you, and leave it to grow. Act as if the money does not exist.

Eventually, you will notice that those seemingly small decisions not to spend, such as not eating out at an expensive restaurant, switching the bulb in your home to energy efficient bulbs, and taking the subway instead of getting a cab – has helped you accumulate a significant amount of money. At the same time helped avoid the tendency of increasing your spending as your income grows. Consequently, you will find yourself having multiple sources of income, receiving regular dividends from that Apple shares you bought, that oil and gas giant, or that industrial conglomerate. You have succeeded in investing in your future.

The application of this calculation can help you determine the payment on a mortgage, your overall retirement planning needs, the amount needed to contribute to college funds, credit cards, and other financial decisions.

Beware of little expenses. A small leak will sink a great ship.

Benjamin Franklin

Bottom Line: The easiest way of knowing the effect of time and interest on your present or future money is through net present value calculation. This can be quite useful in budgeting, contract negotiation and short-term, long-term planning.

CHAPTER SIX

AUTOMATION IS THE SOLUTION

You have a problem, and that's financial procrastination. We have explored how to identify this problem. You even did an introspection and discovered that you are reactive in your financial affairs. Yet, you own business or have plans of owning one. But, you know your attitude towards your finances will ruin you. What do you do? Simple, automation is the solution.

When we talk about automation, what comes to mind? For some people, it is robots taking over human jobs. For others, it is a computer software. Either way, the future promises more rapid and continual change towards automation ever. So, what exactly does it mean?

Automation is the act of implementing the control of equipment (in this case, finance) with advanced technology.

AUTOMATION IS INEVITABLE

Here's the thing. A couple of years ago, a research was carried out by analysts at Oxford University in collaboration with consultants at Deloitte. The result of this study, which was quite disturbing to finance professionals, revealed that there is a 95% likelihood that chartered accountants will lose their jobs to some form of automation, two decades from now. Of course, this is based on the nature of work they do, and the continuous advancement in technology.

As disconcerting as this analysis is, one can say that it is long overdue. Because the average number of the full-time employee has started declining from 119 people for every $1.9 Billion to 71 since 2004. A consulting firm, Hackett Group, carried out a study to understand why. They discovered that one of the reasons for this decline is due to the increase in the usage of automation within the department of finance.

According to David Reilly, CTO at Bank of America, automation will "change how we insureproperty, loan money, invest money, deliver technology, write research reports, and what professionals in financial services do every day." For example, an insurance company *can incorporate far more data — from credit scores to behavior — when it decides how risky a customer is...Every week in the news we read about a new application for artificial intelligence, machine learning, neural networks, or robots — whether it is self-driving cars, AI assistants, predictive models, robots building (or printing) hardware, or how to invest our money ... Put these all in the category of automation — and that is what will impact finance the most in the next decade."*

As far as automation is concerned, not only are finance executives sure of their aptness at identifying opportunities to utilize it (automation) within a particular department, they also reported knowing how to implement it. And, they are quite eager to. Based on data from a survey by The Economist Intelligence on business leaders in the US and western Europe, sixty –two percent of finance executives have the intention of increasing automation in their department in less than twenty-four months.

Automation is not really a new thing in the world of finance. According to the United States Institute of Management Accountants (IMA), there were some firms using information technology to automate their financial processes as far back as 1997.

WHY SHOULD YOU EMBRACE AUTOMATION?

"If you are not for us, then you are against us." As far as automation goes, this quote is quite accurate. If you don't embrace automation, your only other option is to protect your business against it. This is a bad idea. Yes, people are going to lose their job because of this advancement. However, that is common with most social changes. There is always a period of painful transition. By perceiving automation as a negative force and protecting your business against it, your competitions will surpass you, and you will lose the very business you were trying to protect in the first place.

Automation can really be a positive tool that can help with monotonous jobs, jobs that people find inherently boring, and help workers to develop, explore, and do things they truly enjoy. However, this can only happen after short-term pain. According to business optimization strategist Darnyelle A. Jervey, CEO of Incredible One Enterprises, "automated systems in small business can make success predictable and allow you to focus on what's important."

One of the major benefits of automating is that it gets easier for you to track results and estimate how things to do to make your time more productive. This will help grow your business in the long run. It takes administrative tasks off your plate and leaves you to concentrate on what's important—working with clients and business development marketing to get new clients.

No computer is going to replace human creativity. Social interaction cannot be done using a computer, or even the process of making those big chunks of money.

The point here is to automate your business so much as to allow yourself concentrate on whatever it is you love doing. Whether it is shaking the hand of your clients, planning your long-term vision, designing that next revolutionary product or service or spending more time with your staff. Because regardless of the amount of automation you integrate into your business, it's the people behind those systems that matter most.

"You're either the one that creates the automation or you're getting automated."

Tom Preston-Werner

Bottom Line: You are a lucky financial procrastinator. Gone are the days when you were required to travel all the way down to your bank, spend precious time to wait in line, and sit down with a financial adviser to talk about your financial future. Those are things of the past. For many, they are becoming archaic. You no longer have an excuse to be a poor procrastinator. All you have to do is embrace automation.

CHAPTER SEVEN

NOW IS THE TIME TO INVEST IN YOUR FUTURE

Take a deep breath, close your eyes and imagine yourself. Ten, maybe twenty years from now, where do you see yourself?

That question was not rhetorical. Keep your eyes closed, and say the answer out loud. You will either like or hate the answer depending on where you are, and what you are doing right now. You'll only like the answer you hear if you are investing in your future. At the end of it all, who doesn't want to have a good future?

You don't have to answer that. It's glaring enough that everyone desires. However, for us to get this good future we so desperately crave, we must first acknowledge the part we have to play to get it. Basically, the only person who determines if you have a good future is you. It will not be taken care of. Not by good fortune, not by circumstances, and certainly not by someone else. You must act now.

Without any doubt, investing in your future is the most important goal you can have. To attain this lofty goal, a level of sacrifice in the present is required. This can involve dedicating not just your time, but also your mental energy and cash into an investment whose return is not instant. Yet, battling with the uncertainty. Not knowing if said investment will ever prove valuable.

Unfortunately, a large percentage of the population do not bother to invest in their future. Apart from sheer ignorance, other reasons people are not interested in investing in the future include; financial procrastination, being reactive in matters of finance, and the inability to comprehend how time affects the value of money.

As such, they are not equipped to handle difficult financial situations. No one is saying you have to turn into some type of Warren Buffet to secure your future. You don't even have to save 80%+ of your income. That would just be insane. However, start by saving what you can. Stop eating out, and stop going on a shopping spree, buying things you don't really need. Most importantly, stop trying to convince yourself that the stuff you buy is some sort of compensation for the horrible things you had to go through during the week.

Two Essential Principles of Investing In Your Future

1. Start Early

Whatever the investment you intend to venture into, be it ownership investment, fixed-income investment, mutual fund investing, or tax-deferred investment, an important principle is to start early.

You shouldn't wait till you run into some unfortunate circumstance. Do not wait until you are out of job. Knowing that it takes time to build something, you should start now, while the going is good.

You can start by building an alternative income stream that you can rely on. If you start now, by the time you need it, sometime in the future, your investment would there to care for you.

2. It is a Long-term Game

Investing in the future is a long-term thing. Consequently, you have to be in for the long term. This means you cannot be interested in instant gratification. While I understand the difficulty in spending your precious time and money on investment, knowing that the return is not immediate, it's also important for you to understand that If you don't, your progress will be slow. The future would creep up on you, and you wouldn't be ready.

BEFORE YOU START INVESTING

Investing can be scary, and daunting to anybody (No pressure, it's only your future that is at stake here). But, it needn't be like that. Here are some things you should keep in mind as you think about venturing into the world of investing.

What if you know nothing about investments?

Hard as it is to believe, you're not alone in this. Knowledge of the differences between stocks and bonds, or an IRA and a Roth IRA was not wired into anyone's DNA at birth. Just do some research. Start with the basics so you'll have a comfortable working knowledge of key investment principles, then build on your knowledge over time. Start by googling financial terms that you don't understand. Next, consider possible investment options, and settle for one or more that might work for you.

Not all investments are created equal

According to research, tolerance for risk differs, depending on the age and gender of the said investor. However, this is no reason not to invest. If you do your research well, you'll find out that some investments are less volatile and more conservative than others. Pick your investment based on how comfortable you are with the risk, and keeping in mind your long-term goal.

You don't need a truckload of cash

Jack didn't know what he would invest in yet, but he knew he wanted to invest. However, he was waiting for the big bucks, the huge payday that would never come. It was too late when he realized his mistake, he should have just invested every little dollar he got.

Perhaps one of the biggest misconceptions in investing for the future is that it's only for folks that have a huge sum of money resting in a bank account. You can make your investments based on your budgets along with your savings, rent, and utilities. You have an option of investing through a retirement plan. Another option is to set up an investment plan, in which you would compel yourself to invest a particular amount every month. Invest in your future, don't be like Jack.

"You cannot save time for future use. But you can invest it for the future you."

Bottom Line: If at some point, you need a little guidance, get the service of a financial advisor. Get someone that understands your goals, someone that can alleviate your fear, someone that will help protect your future.

It doesn't really matter how you start. Whether you are starting small, or big, doing it by yourself or hiring an advisor, just as long as you are doing something. As long as you are investing in your future.

CHAPTER EIGHT

ARE YOU A POOR PROCRASTINATOR?

I guess that's the question you have been asking yourself. It was the reason you picked up this book, it was the reason you read it this far. You were hoping somewhere along the way; you would find the answer to the question. You probably did find the answer you were searching for, but you're still in denial. It's time to remove that blindfold. Look yourself in the mirror and ask, "Am I a poor procrastinator?"

Let's answer that question together, shall we?

According to Gregory Schraw, Theresa Wadkins, and Lori Olafson, three criteria must be met before a behavior can be classified as procrastination. These criteria are;

1.   Counterproductive: Procrastination tends to hinder the achievement of a goal.

2.   Needless: There is absolutely no reason to put off what you are supposed to do.

3.   Delaying: It causes you to act later than planned or scheduled.

Based on these three criteria, procrastination can be defined as the act of voluntarily delaying an intended course of action despite expecting to be worse off for the delay (Steel 2001). What you need to understand is that putting a task off for a rational reason is not procrastination. Apart from the key element of delay, the irrationality of the delay is another thing to consider when defining procrastination.

TYPES OF PROCRASTINATORS

The Avoider

If you delay tasks just because of the discomfort, unpleasantness, or high stakes associated with such task, you are an avoider. According to Erica Jong, "we are so scared of being judged that we look for every excuse to procrastinate." Avoiders tend to worry too much about what other people think. As such, rather than failing, they avoid doing the task altogether.

The Perfectionist

They are like the opposite of avoiders. They set unrealistic goals for themselves. Their standards are always so high that they get overwhelmed and never finish. The Renaissance artist, Leonardo da Vinci is a classic example of a perfectionist procrastinator.

The Indecisive Procrastinator

As the name implies, these types of procrastinators simply can't decide. They avoid the responsibility of decision making so they wouldn't be blamed for the negative outcome they anticipate.

The Thrill-seeker

The adrenaline junkie procrastinator. This type of person is addicted to the rush he or she gets from completing things at the last minute. The thrill seeker feels he or she thrives under pressure. However, such person will not be able to accomplish his or her full potential. The work might get done, but it won't be the best he or she can do.

The Busy Procrastinator

The busy procrastinator creates a checklist of every task he or she intends to do. However, because of the length of the checklist, he does too few. Rather than the nature of the task (as in the perfectionist), the length of the task gets overwhelming that he or she will always fail to finish.

WHAT IF YOU ARE A POOR PROCRASTINATOR?

After much introspection, you discovered that you are in fact a poor procrastinator. So, what? Big deal. Doesn't mean you are not capable of changing; doesn't mean you are not capable of investing in your financial future. Here is what you should do.

Accept That There is no Perfect Time

Start by compelling yourself from ever using the words "I just don't feel like it right now." This is an excuse that has ruined your life in many ways than one. It is the way you justify putting off till tomorrow what you can easily do today.

The truth is you will never feel like it. There is never a perfect time to face that difficult task you have been avoiding. You are looking for a temporary reprieve, forgetting that the keyword here is "temporary." Regardless of how bad your finances are, avoiding it will definitely not make it any better.

By accepting that your level of motivation can never be equal to the task at hand, you can finally stop using the excuse, "I just don't feel like it right now." Instead, start using these three words, "Just get started."

Commit to Just 5 Minutes of Your Time.

The three words "Just get started" literally mean what you think it means, just gets started. It doesn't matter how long (for now), just start the work even if it's for five minutes. This is how it works. When you reduce the time you are dedicating to the task in your head, it gets easier to make the first move. You can pull out a pen and, paper, boot up your computer, and log into your bank account.

According to Amy Morin, author of "13 Things Mentally Strong People Don't Do," "We spend three days dreading a task that might take 30 minutes." The thing is, you will realize that once you get started, the discomfort that is a result of fear or nervousness goes away. It's not so different from working out. Once you start, you'll realize it's not so bad. Also, our confidence in our ability to get things done increases.

Make All Your Deadlines Feel 'Present'

This is especially useful to the thrill-seeking procrastinator. We set tasks that are realistic, only to wait until the last minute to start. If you file your taxes on April 15, you are totally in this category.

The question now we need to ask ourselves is, why do we find it so hard to stick to deadlines? The answer may lie in how we categorize time in our minds.

According to analysis, individuals have the tendency of viewing task completion in one of two ways.

1. As happening right now.
2. As happens in the future.

When we view all our tasks as happening right now, we become more proactive. We become motivated to initiate an action towards it. So, start setting your deadlines based on your own present time, maybe a week to the actual deadline, and you will beat deadlines.

Break Your Goals intoa Manageable Size

This is quite easy. When your goals are too big or too vague, they can be difficult to manage. Break it down into concrete, manageable pieces. Set short-term goals that will ultimately help you attain your long-term goals.

Example, if your goal is to buy a house. Make the goal less vague by knowing the exact price for the house you would be buying and how much it would cost. Next, break it down into manageable pieces by exploring different investment options. You can further break it down by putting some money away every day.

Reward Yourself

Finally, reward yourself for every task you get done. No, not by getting a reservation in that expensive restaurant, or going on a shopping spree. Forty- five minutes of Netflix drama can serve as the right incentive for doing your taxes. However, if you are putting away money to buy a house, owning the house can serve as the reward.

"Only put off till tomorrow what you are willing to die having left undone."

Pablo Picasso

Bottom line: Restructure your daily life and environment to account for the newly gained perspective. Not only do you have to discipline yourself, but you also have to be capable of motivating yourself. That shouldn't be difficultbecause it's only your future that's at stake. It's time to stop being a poor procrastinator, start investing in your future now.

CHAPTER 9

WHO ARE THE INVESTED MILLENNIALS?

THE TRAITS OF AN INVESTED MILLENNIAL

James graduated from college armed with not just a degree, but determination. He had a resolve to succeed, and a fierce need to attain financial freedom. He didn't want to be like his father, who worked in the mines all his life, and was eventually killed by the work he did. James knew he had to get proactive about his finance to avoid his father's fate. However, there were two problems. He had a student loan to pay and had no idea what to invest in. That never stopped him.

James started his journey towards financial freedom with a decision to be financially proactive. He didn't let his debt deter him. Rather, he used it to fuel his determination. James used the memory of his father's slavery to push himself towards the financial freedom he craved.

His first step involved ending the bad habit of procrastinating in affairs of finance. He understood now how much it cost him in dollars. He learned how the time value of money affected his financial life, and how to act in view of that. Eventually, he explored different investment options, with the knowledge of the essential principles of investing. James acquired the knowledge necessary to make informed investments and acted on it. When he finally got a job that paid enough for him to invest in bonds, stocks, and real estate, he invested in himself and his future. He invested in his freedom, and eventually settled his student loan.

James had transitioned from a poor procrastinator to an Invested Millennial. He was just twenty-two years old.

This part of the book focuses on your own transformation from a poor procrastinator to an Invested Millennial. If you have stayed with me this far in the book, then you already know who a poor procrastinator is. So, you are wondering right now if you are an Invested Millennial? What does the word "Millennial" even mean? Here is all you need to know.

Who are Millennials?

Based on the definition in the Merriam-Webster Dictionary, the word Millennial is used to describe a generation of people born between the early 1980s and 1990s. However, the year bracket has been extended to include children born in the early 2000s. Some scholars even added a year as recent as 2004 into the bracket.

"Millennials" refers to folks that were born near or came of age at the beginning of the 21st century. They were the first to be born into a digital world. As such, the dependence on technology to function in their everyday lives goes without saying.

Millennials were raised in a world filled with electronics, social media, and social networks. More than any other generation, Millennials have received a significant amount of marketing attention. While the media were trying to sell one product or another to these set of people, their parents were trying to sell a little confident. Using mantras such as "You are special" and "follow your dreams," the parents managed to instill confidence in the Millennials. This is a good thing, right?

Maybe not so much. Even though confidence in itself is a good thing, overconfidence has created a generation of narcissism and entitlement. A study revealed that Millennials are slightly more optimistic about the future of the United States of America than any generation before. However, the fact still remains that, they are the first generation since the Silent Generation (the 1950s to early

1960s) expected to be less financially successful than their parents. Do you want to know the reason?

The effect of the great recession, which resulted in high levels of unemployment among young people, has been speculated to have lasting economic damage for this generation. Aside from the influence of the great depression, Millennials are expected to be less financially successful because of the trait of an average member of this generation of people. Let me explain further.

An Average Millennial

Millennials have been described in several ways. They have been described as lazy and narcissistic. They are unable to hold a job long, jumping from one job to another. According to "Trophy Kids," a book written by Ron Alsop, because many young people have been rewarded for minimal accomplishments, such as mere participation in competitive sports, they have developed unrealistic expectations of working life.

They demand more flexible work schedules, they indulge their narcissistic tendencies by demanding more "me time" on the job, continuous feedback, and career advice (they probably won't use) from managers.

An article in "Time" published in May 2013 said, "They're narcissistic. They're lazy. They're coddled. They're even a bit delusional. Those aren't just unfounded negative stereotypes about 80 million Americans born roughly between 1980 and 2000. They're backed up by a decade of sociological research."

Another study that was published in 2012, based on the analysis of nine million high school seniors that were divided into two databases, described Millennials as "more civically and politically disengaged, more focused on materialistic values, and less concerned about helping the larger community than were Generation X (born 1962-1981) and Baby Boomers (born 1946 to about 1961) at the same ages." The current trend of Millennials focuses more on extrinsic values such as money, fame, and image. They are less interested in intrinsic values such as self-acceptance, group affiliation, and community.

The financial issues experienced by Millennials include:

Not Having Enough for Living Expenses

The most popular financial problem Millennials experience is not having enough money for day-to-day living. This is primarily due to high unemployment rate. It is also partly whyMillennials putoff working to further their education. Some young people do part-time work, and those that get an entry-level job have to settle for very measly pay.

Consequently, most Millennials are more concerned about surviving rather than living, they are more concerned with the present, not the future.

Not Able to Attain Financial Freedom

Studies show that Millennials depend on their parents for financial support longer than any previous generation. Those that don't live from paycheck-to-paycheck. This makes it rather difficult for Millennials to attain financial freedom.

Debt

According to Pew Research Center, about 37% of the households headed by Millennials have some student debt to pay, the average debt being about $13,000. Those with no student debt have accumulated about nine times as much wealth as debtor households ($10,900 vs. $1,200). This is true despite the fact that debtors and non-debtors have nearly identical household incomes in each group. The prevalent unemployment and low-paying jobs don't make paying the debts any easier.

A viable option for getting out of debt and investing in your future is to extend the payment of your student debt to reduce your monthly payment. This would leave you with some extra cash which you can put in your retirement account.

You need to understand that being in debt is not really a bad thing as long as you know how to manage it. Installment debts when paid on time, can help you establish a good credit score which can come in handy if you ever need a bank loan.

Saving for a Big Purchase

A huge sum of money is required as down payment to make huge purchases such as a house. Unfortunately for most Millennials, between paying college loan, credit card debts, and being underpaid, the down payment is not within their means.

At some time in history, it was considered profitable to save money in savings account, but not anymore. Between the interest rate that can't keep up with inflation, and the maintenance fees paid to banks, Millennials are losing money this way. The bank might be a safe place to keep your emergency fund, but it is not a smart place to save for big purchases anymore.

Planning for the future

For a generation that has watched their parents and grandparents financial struggle, Millennials appear to have a casual attitude towards retirement planning. At a glance, we would blame this growing trend on their "live at the moment" lifestyle.

However, a deeper analysis would reveal how difficult it is for young people to put money aside. The retirement savings plans are now tied to employers, and contributions are voluntary. Not everyone has access to an employer-provided plan, and those that do would consider themselves lucky if the employer contributes anything. Let's not forget the thousands of dollars of student loan still waiting to be paid.

The studies show how we can appreciate what it means to be an average Millennial, and why you are expected to fail financially. However, the subsequent chapters will help you understand how to change this terrible destiny, and how to achieve more. You will be equipped with the tools you need to become an Invested Millennial.

An Invested Millennial

The traits of an Invested Millennial are numerous. Nevertheless, for the purpose of brevity, we narrowed it down into four. They are:

- Having clear goals in life
- They value in themselves
- On the way or have attained financial freedom
- Contributing to society

Note: It might have occurred to you that you are not within the age bracket described as Millennials. Maybe you are a Generation X, or a Baby Boomer, no worries. As long as financial independence is what you seek, this book is for you. Don't you dare drop it, you'll end up regretting it.

"If you don't design your own life plan, chances are you'll fall into someone else's plan. And guess what they have planned for you? Not much."

Jim Rohn

CHAPTER 10

TRAIT #1: HAVING CLEAR GOALS IN LIFE

The first trait of an Invested Millennial is that; they have a clear goal in life. We already know what goals are. Though, it is difficult to put into clear words. It is when an overweight person decides to lose fifty pounds within a timeframe, and does so. An athlete decides to reduce the time spent running a hundred meters by .05 seconds. In finance, goals are usually in the form of a plan of attaining financial freedom within a particular period.

According to Advanced English Dictionary, goals can be defined as the state of affairs that a plan is intended to achieve and that (when achieved) terminates behavior intended to achieve it.

IMPORTANCE OF HAVING CLEAR GOALS IN LIFE

1. Having Clear Goals Helps Push Us

When we write out what we intend to achieve with a set date for such accomplishment, it gives us a purpose. A goal written down gives us something to plan and work for. The emphasis here is placed on the word "Written" because an external representation of our desire is required to serve as a constant reminder of the direction we intend to go in life. Writing out our goals reminds us of things we are yet to achieve.

Another major reason you should write out your goals is that; it helps you avoid the "goal setting cycle" we're all too familiar with. You know it already, don't you?

You pick a goal

You get excited

You start working on it

Motivation wanes,

You lose interest

You abandon the goal

It's time for you to break this cycle, all you need is a pen and a piece of paper. When you have goals that you can visualize, it becomes easier to connect yourself with your inner desire. Consequently, when your motivation starts to wane, all you must do is look at that piece of paper, and your motivation will be renewed.

2. Setting Clear Goals Makes Our Aspirations Less Daunting

Citing the example from the last chapter, James had a goal of becoming financially independent. He started by breaking down this intimidating aspiration into small manageable goals. The first manageable goal was a simple decision to run an automated savings account, all the way to make the complex decision of what real estate investment was right for him.

A lot of us have dreams that appear impossible to achieve. This can be quite discouraging. However, a properly set goal can help break these daunting desires into manageable pieces. The small pieces are more achievable and are easier to act upon. It makes it easier to draw a definite plan and can serve as a source of motivation when achieved.

3. Goals Help Us Believe in Ourselves

John F. Kennedy had an impossible goal. He believed that his country would be the first to land on the moon. His famous address of "landing a man on the moon and returning him safely to the Earth" which he proposed to Congress in 1961 was an inspiration to a whole nation. Eight years later, Kennedy's impossible goal was achieved when Neil Armstrong and Buzz Aldrin landed their Lunar Module and walked on the Moon.

Goal setting can be described as a form of inspiration; it helps us believe we can achieve what we thought was impossible. This is a way of fueling our ambition and demanding more from ourselves. Goal setting helps us accomplish things that a lot of people can only dream of, but only a few accomplish.

4. Goals Help Us Evaluate Our Shortcoming

Concrete goals with a timeline that are not attained within the allotted time can be quite frustrating. However, the fact that we plotted a course towards achieving this goal makes it possible to appraise. We can evaluate the path taken, to get a better understanding of why we failed in the first place. We can re-assess decisions and purchases made, or indecision and purchases not made. There is always a second chance to plot a better course towards attaining our goals.

5. Goals Tell You What You Truly Want

Occasionally, we set goals without knowing what we really want. For example, in other to experience a vague sense of financial accomplishment you can decide to purchase a convertible BMW you don't really need, to make up for what you actually want; financial comfort. Though your brand-new car might project the opposite, you'll know in your heart that you are broke, yet spent all your savings buying a car.

If you don't set goals, you might become one of those people that walk around in life with a muddled notion of what success and achievement really mean.

By writing out our goals, we are indirectly asking ourselves what we really want in life. And as our wants changes, we can constantly re-assess our goals to ensure we are on the right track.

6. Goals Help Us Live Life to the Fullest

You got a two weeks' vacation to Italy, you and your family. With so many things to experience, so many landmarks to visit, what would you do? Would you research the interesting sights, things to experience, and landmarks to visit, and arrange the order of visit? Or would you just wander around Italy, hoping to stumble upon that famous leaning tower?

Your life is not so different from the illustration above. In order to live it to the fullest and maximize time, you have to draw out where you expect yourself to be at different moments in time. This doesn't necessarily mean that you should plan every single moment of your life. No, it only ensures that you don't find yourself wandering, and wondering exactly where you are heading.

KNOWING THE PURPOSE OF THEIR EXISTENCE

I know what you are thinking. The answer is no, your purpose and your goals are not the same. The fact that they are interlinked makes it difficult to tell them apart. However, the major difference between your goal and your purpose is the time frame. To reach your goal, a time frame is required. Purpose, being the reason you want to achieve a goal, requires no time frame. Basically, there must be a purpose behind every goal you set.

The interesting thing about having clear goals in life is that; you also understand your purpose. The knowledge of one's purpose is something everyone tries to understand, but few really do. This is usually due to an inability to commit to the desired outcome. However, invested Millennials have mastered this part. Not only do they understand the purpose of their existence, they fully commit themselves to this purpose. There are a few simple steps that can help commit to a purpose, and in extension, a goal.

1. Determine what your purpose is

This is probably the most difficult part of committing to a purpose. The first question you have to ask yourself is "What do I want to be doing thirty years from now." To make it easier, you could pick a particular purpose in different areas of your life.

2. Set goals that will ultimately help fulfill your purpose

After you have determined what your purpose is, it gets more challenging. Sticking with that particular purpose can be quite difficult. What do you do? All you have to do is set your goals with the purpose in mind. Therefore, with every goal you achieve, you get one step closer to fulfilling your purpose.

3. Write down your purpose

Like your goal, you also need to write down your purpose. It's a way of telling your brain how serious the commitment you are making is. It also gives you a clarity of purpose.

4. Keep reminding yourself of your purpose

By constantly reminding yourself of your purpose, you get the momentum to keep going on. Reminding yourself of your purpose can serve as a motivation. You don't have to whisper "I have a purpose" every hour, that'll just be crazy. You can start by surrounding yourself with people that are aligned with your purpose. Your environment, even the desktop background of your laptop should remind you of your purpose.

5. Do one thing every day that brings you closer to your purpose

Make sure you do one thing every day that takes you closer to your goal, and ultimately your purpose. It doesn't really matter if it's ten minutes or ten hours. Work on your goal every day, and fulfilling your purpose is certain.

SEEK AFTER A LIFE ASCENDING JOURNEY

The need to seek a life ascending journey is fundamental to every human. However, very few actually do. It's a desire that originates from demanding a higher standard from yourself. Millennials on a life ascending journey constantly use the mantra "I shall do better." They demand personal freedom from their life. The journey helps them get rid of fearful thoughts, and a need to fit in. They are no longer afraid of standing out.

1. Healthy Choice of Relationship

Invested Millennials seek a healthy choice of relationships. Although they understand the dangers of standing alone in life, they are still picky about people they get involved with. They expect to be loved and respected in any relationship they get involved in and freely give it (love and respect) in return.

They demand the same standards in others as they do themselves, and trust that their loved ones can live up to these standards. Most importantly, they understand that family isn't always blood.

2. They Focus on Possibilities Not Problems

Invested Millennials have a solution-focused approach to problem-solving. Consequently, they engage all creative processes in solving problems. They think laterally, deriving confidence from the deep belief that every problem has an available solution.

However, when the solution seems elusive, they are never too proud to seek the opinion of others.

3. They Develop Themselves

A life ascending journey is impossible without self-development. Invested Millennials constantly adjust their personal beliefs, knowledge, and skill to avoid complacency. This is the only way they can meet the higher standards they set for themselves. They decidedly stay away from habits and people that hold back their personal development.

4. They manage their time wisely

Invested Millennials always get things done on time. They deal with the big important things before focusing on the little ones and never get distracted by small, unimportant tasks. Most importantly, they do not procrastinate.

They not only respect their own time; they also respect others'. Consequently, they never attend any event late, and always meet their deadlines.

5. They take responsibility for their actions

Invested Millennials that have embarked on a life ascending journey always take responsibility for their actions. They understand that it's the best route to the development of personal power. Ability to take responsibility for one's actions (both positive and negative), allows one to learn from a mistake. Therefore, investing Millennials see mistakes as a self-created learning experience.

A Millennial on a life-ascending journey is humble enough to understand the value of making mistakes.

6. Invested Millennials Are Kind

They are good to themselves and to the people they love. Their life ascending journey makes them understand that the power of kindness is the greatest value you can offer as a human being.

"People with clear, written goals, accomplish far more in a shorter period of time than people without them could ever imagine."

Brian Tracy

Bottom Line: On their life-ascending journey, Invested Millennials have embraced their right to think for themselves, and to speak their mind. Most importantly, they have earned the right to pursue happiness, success and financial gain without apologizing for it.

CHAPTER 11

TRAIT #2 THEY VALUE IN THEMSELVES

Jane Smith was a Southern girl who never attended an Ivy League college. In fact, she graduated from a community college. However, she made a pact with her dead grandmother that she would continue to learn, she promised she would continue to grow. Jane Smith was determined to break the proverbial glass ceiling, which she believed held her mother back in life.

So, Jane improved herself every opportunity she got. She attended night classes and wrote exams, till she landed a job that paid her six figures. Jane was not complacent. She continued to invest in herself. She spent thousands of dollars on her financial education. And lost thousands more trying out what she had learned. She invested in stocks, commodities, and real estate. She even invested in art.

Jane Smith became more than a girl with a community college degree. She became a competitive product with features, assets, and liabilities. Like a product, she improved upon these features each year until she became unique. The southern girl became a brand.

Invested Millennials assign a value to themselves, they never leave it to chance. This is the second trait you need to acquire as an Invested Millennial. You need to learn to think of yourself as a product that needs constant improvements, to remain relevant in the market. It doesn't have to be an expensive upgrade like attending a business school. No, there are other cheap, yet effective ways of upgrading yourself, less expensive ways of making yourself more valuable as an employee as you progress through your career.

An example is reading a book. Yes, it's that easy. You can pick one topic to read that is relevant to your career path and read six books about it each year. For example, you can begin by reading about communication techniques. Now imagine, ten, twenty years from the time you started how you would become an authority in your chosen field. You'll be amazed at how a small change like this can boost your career and personal life.

Invested Millennials view knowledge as a lifelong pursuit. They are the women that return to college after raising three kids, to pursue a different career path. The business professional, who obtains additional certification to push himself forwards in his niche. Invested Millennials are people that place value on themselves, and invest heavily to increase that value.

INVESTED MILLENNIALS INVEST IN THEMSELVES.

The term "Invested Millennials" speaks for itself. It refers to a group of people who commit money, time, energy, or effort into developing themselves with the expectation of some worthwhile result. Pretty straightforward, right? Let us consider the ways in which Millennials invest in themselves.

They Invest in Their Financial Literacy

Financial illiteracy is arguably the root of all financial struggles. The risk you take when investing reduces significantly if you understand exactly what you are doing. Consequently, the greatest investment you can make is in your financial education.

Imagine for a moment that you ran into a small fortune, maybe inherited some money from an uncle you didn't know you had. So, you decided to invest it on your own, even though you have the same level of financial education as a newborn baby. People around you were investing in a small startup company, and you joined the bandwagon. The reward looked quite attractive. Also, the broker told you it was the right move to make. He told you a hundred people had invested already, and a hundred more were waiting too.

You invested heavily, putting every penny you had on the startup company, and even invited your family and friends to invest. "It's a once in a lifetime deal," you told them.

So, you went to sleep. That night, you dreamed of the millions of dollars you were about to make. However, the shrill sound of your phone woke you at midnight, it was your broker. He wanted to be the first to tell you, he said. The startup tech company you invested all your money, the one you blindly put your future in, had declared bankruptcy. You are once again penniless, he concluded.

Okay, let's return to the present. The truth is, with your level of financial education, the probability of making money from that investment is at best, 50 – 50. The risk taken in any business increases with the cluelessness of the investor, that's you.

Most people never learn from their bad investment experience because they are unwilling to admit that their lack of knowledge caused them to lose money. Rather, they blame it on the investment itself. They make statements like "the company was mismanaged," as a justification of their ignorance. Thus, they end up trapped in a cycle of bad investments.

Financial literates make their investments when the market is down, and exit at the peak. The financial dimwits, encouraged by the rising prices, buy when it is high. Then, they ride the wave all the way down to the bottom, hoping to recover some of their investment. They make investments based on greed and exit out of fear. Invest in your financial education, don't be a dimwit.

You might ask, what if you have other passions besides stocks, bonds and all that? My advice, learn the financial aspect of your passion, understand it, and invest in it. Turn your personal passion into a project. If you love baking, learn the financial aspect. If you love writing, find a way of making money off it. That is the foundation on which successful companies are built, on financial literacy.

They Invest Their Money Wisely

Invested Millennials, like most other investors, put their money in traditional investments. However, they do this based on the faith they have in the knowledge they have acquired. They understand that success in traditional investments is dependent on the success of the entire market. Although financial literacy helps manage the risk of traditional investments, there are still some downfalls that are because of time and control.

1. Stocks

Investment in stocks is the most popular form of investment among traditional investors. It basically involves paying for a share of stock. In return, you (the investor) are entitled to part of the profit in the form of dividend and price appreciation. The average price-earning for a stock is between $7 and $30. However, the downside of this type of investment occurs when you buy high, and you have to watch it fall.

2. Commodities

A commodity is an economic good, such as a product of agriculture or mining. They are valuable. However, the value associated with commodities is simply a reflection of their scarcity, they do not produce value on their own. The more available they are, the cheaper they become.

The price of gold, crude oil, and other commodities are in a constant flux. Therefore, they may not be a solid option for long-term investment. In fact, the value of crude oil could completely crash as the demand for cleaner sources of energy increases.

While investing in commodities outside the United States might look like a good idea, the interest rates point to the dollar getting stronger.

3. Real estate

Real estate is property consisting of land and the buildings on it, along with its natural resources such as crops, mineral or water. It goes without saying that, the business aspect involves the buying, selling, or renting of real estate.

This is one of the few investments in which you (the investor) can leverage equity, in return for more profit. The only problem with this type of leverage is that you own less. Someone out there is borrowing a majority.

The major downside of real estate investment is that a miniscule change in the marketplace can leave you penniless.

4. Startups

Startups are entrepreneurial ventures which are typically newly emerged, fast-growing business that aims to meet a marketplace need by developing a viable business model around an innovative product, service, process or a platform. That's Wikipedia's definition, and it's quite long. Let me give you a shorter version; startups are companies just starting up.

Startups investment is not exactly the same as normal stocks. When you invest in startups, you get the opportunity to buy a larger stake in the company. The startup owners are usually passionate about their brand. While this may attract a lot of attention, investing in startups is a gamble. You would be giving your money to untested ideas and entrepreneurs.

5. Invest in your passion

The four investments described above are the easiest ways of claiming financial success (we'll discuss this further in another chapter). However, they give very little room for personal growth because you have to depend on other people most of the time.

Time spent investing in your own passion can be quite rewarding, and can lead to true financial success in the long run. You not only experience personal growth, but you will also be much happier for it. There's a feeling of "being in control" associated with this type of investment, which increases the emphasis on financial literacy. Turn your passion into a brand!

"Until you value yourself, you won't value your time. Until you value your time, you will not do anything with it."

M. Scott Peck

Bottom Line: In your quest to become an Invested Millennial, you must increase your own personal value. Increasing your value goes beyond the financial (though, it's important). It also involves increasing your knowledge, investing in what you love (your passion), and investing in who you love (you). At the end of it all, you'll not only be making money, but you'll also become a better person for it.

Chapter 12

Trait #3: On the way / Have Attained Financial Freedom

Everyone called Mark a geek, but he didn't mind. Labels gave people a sense of organization and belonging in college, and Harvard was no different, he told himself. They were not altogether wrong; he was a geek. He preferred staying in his dorm room on Saturday nights writing codes, rather than hanging with the guys. Mark would spend weeks working on his computer and developing websites just for the fun of it. To his close friends, Mark was a gifted programmer. To everyone else, he was just a geek.

Mark decided to turn his passion into a brand, create something that would last. So he built a social media platform for Harvard and called it The FaceBook. He wanted a place on the internet where Harvard undergrads would be able to interact. It was a huge success.

Not only was the social media platform popular among Harvard students, but Mark also extended the service to the whole world. By 2012, Mark's social media platform had one billion users. He invested in himself, and his passion. Personal fulfillment was the return of that investment.

Everyone called Mark Zuckerberg a geek, but he didn't mind. The geek has attained financial freedom; he is now worth $71.5 Billion.

What is financial freedom?

Financial freedom occurs when you have sufficient personal wealth to live, without having to work actively for the basic necessities of life. According to Robert Kiyosaki, It's the freedom to be who you really are and do what you really want in life.

You don't have to build a social media platform like Mark Zuckerberg or be a CEO of a huge Tech Company to attain financial freedom. Like Invested Millennials, if the income generated by your asset annually is greater than your annual expense, you are well on your way towards financial freedom.

For example, if you have a quarterly expense of $4,000 and receive a quarterly rent, or dividend of $5,000, while still having other investment, you are on the right path. In other to fully grasp what financial freedom truly means, your assets (anything of value that can be liquidated if you are in debt) and your liability (Homes and automobiles with no liens or mortgages) must be taken into consideration.

There are three important steps that Invested Millennials take towards attaining financial freedom. They are:

1. Having a strong financial foundation
2. Having multiple streams of income, not multiple sources of debt
3. Sought after sustainable passive income (keywords: abundance, security, growth)

HAVING STRONG FINANCIAL FOUNDATIONS

Your financial life could be a tiny little house that won't be able to withstand a light breeze, or it could be a mansion that'll remain standing after a hurricane. It all depends on the type of foundation you have. Your financial foundation serves the purpose of a shock absorber when hit by the turbulence of financial crisis. It's quite simple, do you want to attain financial freedom? Then start building a strong financial foundation. Take these steps to start building a foundation that'll last you a lifetime.

It is important for you to track your expense first, know where all that money is going to. By doing this, you'll be able to save some money by knowing exactly what to cut back. So, here is what you should do, write down everything.

At the beginning of the month, start writing down all the expense you incur. It doesn't matter how big or little, write it down. Your rent/mortgage, payroll deductions, groceries, even a bottle of beer, write it all down. Categorize it, and add it all up at the end of the month. Then calculate your income. It shouldn't be too difficult if you don't have any investment.

Finally, subtract your expenses from your income. For example, if you got a monthly income of $4000, and your calculated expense is $3,500, you'd have $500 leftover.

You have a picture of your cash flow, and you know where all the money has been going. The question is, will the leftover be enough to build the financial foundation you crave? The best advice I can give you at this point is to cut expense. You'll divert the excess money into something else. Please note that solid financial foundation cannot be driven by frugality. No, you need to increase your income, and we'll talk about that later.

Your financial foundation should be a combination of two fundamental components; insurance and cash reserve. It is that "something else" you are supposed to divert the excess money from the expense cut into. Let us begin by talking a little about how insurance can help you in building your foundation.

Insurance is there to protect you in case of a major loss, most importantly, to protect your family against the risk of losing your lifetime earnings. You already know (and probably have) the basic policies such as health insurance (covers your medical expenses in case of emergencies, plus hospital stays), car insurance (if you own a car), and homeowners'/mortgage insurance. But, it's not enough. For your financial foundation to be rock steady, there are other types of insurance you need to seriously consider. They are:

• **Disability insurance:** The purpose of disability insurance policy is to provide you with a monthly income if you ever get injured, and unable to work. Studies have shown that one out of six people in the United States will suffer an incapacitating condition at some point in their lives, and nearly twice more likely to be injured or incapacitated by some type of ailment than to die during your working years. The bottom line of all the quoted data is that this insurance policy can easily come in handy. Note that, most disability insurance policy has 90 days waiting period until the policy kicks in.

- **Life Insurance:** Life insurance is the policy that protects your survivor in case you suffer a premature death. Now, there is a popular misconception that you only need this policy when you are married or having kids. This is wrong. In truth, you are likely to get a lower rate if you get life insurance when you are young and healthy. Apart from the death benefit received by your survivor in the event you die prematurely, it is also a good way of accumulating cash value. The money can be useful in case of emergencies or opportunities.

- **Property/Casualty Insurance:** Another name for this insurance is liability insurance. As the name implies, liability insurance protects you if you ever get injured by someone who has no insurance, or whose insurance is inadequate. It also protects you if you are legally liable for damage to other people's property, or you are legally responsible for their injury.

The next layer in your foundation involves building a cash reserve. I know what it sounds like, it sounds like I'm asking you to keep actual dollar bills. However, that's not the case. Cash reserve actually refers to assets you have built up in your account (that can easily be accessed within three to five days without penalty) for emergency purpose. The general rule of cash reserve (yes, there's a general rule) is that you should always have three months of your living expense if you are renting, and six months if you own a property. You already know how much your monthly expense is. Go ahead multiply it by three, or six, depending on your living condition.

The reason for the three months- six months' rule is that it takes roughly three months of rent to break a lease. Also, it can take as much as six months to sell a house.

Now you have a steady foundation. You could cement it by investing in your retirement account while focusing on your savings. You have probably read it before. However, if you need to refresh your memory, read the previous chapter again. If not, discover the second step to take towards your financial freedom.

Having Multiple Streams Of Income, Not Multiple Sources Of Debt

You need to reduce your sources of debt, before increasing your sources of income. Let's tackle the debts first, shall we?

I'm not going to start by talking about how your multiple sources of debt is hurting your goal of attaining financial freedom, you already read it. More importantly, you are currently experiencing it. However, I will tell you this truth, the pain is never going to go away if you don't do something about it. Congratulations, you took the first step by reading the book this far. Pay attention, this subsequent step is just as important.

You need to have a clear picture of your debt. Calculate exactly how much you owe and how much interest you are paying. Have you done that?

Now create a payment plan that you can stick with. You already know what's left over after paying your expense, calculate how much you can reasonably pay each month. Don't forget your credit card, if it's incurring too much interest, you can look for a zero-interest credit card deal that suits you, and transfer your balance into it.

After you have a handle on your debts, the next move is to generate multiple streams of income. How can you do this, you ask? Stay with me, we are almost there.

I don't think there is a need to explain what multiple sources of income means, the name sort of speaks for itself. It's when you get more than one of income from different sources. The key word to remember here is "diversification."

You might say that you earn enough, that you don't need another source of income. We both know that's not true, you do want financial freedom, don't you? Here are some the reasons why having multiple sources of income is not entirely a bad idea.

It's easier to produce small income sources than to produce a large one. You can have a weekday job paying $3,000 monthly, and still, make $1000 every weekend offering your service as a graphic artist. That is a total of $7,000 per month.

Here is the thing, you'll have zero risks of being left without any income if you lose your weekday job, and it ensures you never get bored. The interesting thing is, you'll be making more money based on your interests, talents, and passion. What is better than that?

There is a downside though, staying on top of all that tasks might be challenging, but we love a good challenge. Now that you have agreed to do this, let's get right to it.

Get a sheet of paper, and write down what you do for a living. I'll stick with my graphic artist example. The next step is to create four categories under your main job that can serve as a potential source of income outside your main job. The four categories under "graphic artist" are a cartoonist, advertising, photography, and creation of special effects for movies.

It doesn't matter if you are an amateur at any of the four categories, you'll get better at it. Set a time frame to master each category. When you become better, create sub-categories of income sources under the four categories. The sub-categories must include books, courses, merchandise, freelancing, speaking, selling advertising, and affiliate marketing.

Writing books is a way of creating a passive source of income (more on that later). You can write books on any of the categories once, and sell it over and over. A graphic artist can write an eBook on "Special Effect in Movies for Amateurs."

You can create additional income for yourself by teaching any (if not all) of the categories as a course, it can take the form of a webinar or podcast. Another option you can explore is public speaking. Don't forget that you can still make money freelancing, after all, you still have four marketable skills. Affiliate marketing is another great way of generating income; you can start by blogging about your passion.

Finally, you can generate income as a business owner. Create something you can sell out of any of the four categories. A graphic artist can create cool designs that can be printed on shirts, then make money by offering them for sale. After that, all you have to focus on is income stream that can expand your business.

There are a couple of dos and don'ts of setting up multiple streams of income. They are:

1. Set-up one income stream at a time, do not jump into different ideas at the same time. You have to wait until one stream is up and running before setting up another

2. Do not hold on to an income stream that isn't generating money. However, you need to be patient.

3. Do not hold on to an income stream if you hate it.

After you have all your income stream up and running, the final step to take towards attaining financial freedom for you to set up multiple sources of passive income.

SEEK SUSTAINABLE PASSIVE INCOME

The final step Invested Millennials take in their quest for financial freedom. They create a sustainable passive income. As usual, we start from the basics.

The United States Internal Revenue Service (IRS) divided income into three categories. They are active income, passive income, and portfolio income. Some analysts consider portfolio income to be passive, dividend and interest being the passive source.

What is passive income?

According to the IRS outline, passive income is defined as either 'net rental income and income from a business in which the taxpayer does not materially participate,' and in some cases, can include self-charged interest. Putting it in the least technical term, passive income is the money you receive on a regular basis with very little effort on your part.

What does not count as passive income?

- If you own a place and decide to rent it out to a business you own, i.e., self-renting, that doesn't count as 'passive income.' The only condition in which it'll count if the lease had been signed before 1988 in which case you've been grandfathered into having that income being defined as passive.
- Any income gotten from leasing a land does not count as passive income.
- If you invest $5,000 into a candy store with the agreement that the owners would pay you a percentage of earnings, and you contribute in any meaningful way to the sales of the candy, the percentage you receive won't qualify as passive income.

We already know what passive income is not, the question is, what investments qualify as a source of passive income?

1. Investment in Real Estate

Investment in real estate is not really a new thing, but the fact that it is capital intensive makes it difficult to start. However, whether you can buy a small house or a build a huge mall, you'll find out that rental properties are a great way of generating passive income through rents.

2.Own a Portfolio of Dividend-Producing Investments

The dividend producing investments we are referring to here include stocks and bonds, which are great sources of passive income, but there's a catch. You have to invest a lot of money to receive something substantial in dividend. Let me explain.

If the average yield on your portfolio every year is 6%, it means that an investment of $100,000 will only get you an income of $6,000. Therefore, to make $60,000 in dividend in a year, you would need to have $1,000,000 in your account.

3.Earn Royalties from Your Creative Works

It's a nice way of making money from your passion. All you have to do is create original content that appeals to a large percentage of the population, and you'll keep receiving royalty long after you completed it. Also, the knowledge that people value what you have created can give your self-esteem a real boost.

4.Create an App

Millennials are now making a lot of money creating and selling apps. You already know how it works. Create an app, and make it available in the app store for free and business owners get to advertise their products in some part of the app for a particular amount. However, any user that wants an ad-free version of the app would have to pay a stipend. Basically, the more downloads you get, the more money you make. If you are lucky, a bigger tech company could buy you out.

5.Patent Royalty

This is quite similar to receiving a royalty for creative work. Except, in this case, you would be receiving money for what you invented. You don't have to be a scientist to have an invention. It could be a process, a produced beat, or a catchphrase, as long it's your intellectual property, the big businesses are going to pay to use it.

6.Ad Revenue From your Website, Blog, and Social Media

If you own a website or a blog, then you can generate passive income through advertisement. From affiliate marketing to Google AdSense, your Ad revenue options are unlimited. Similarly, if you have strong social media following across your accounts, business owners can pay to advertise their product through your account. This is a great way to turn your passion into a source of passive income.

7.Invest in Businesses

You can also invest in private equity opportunities in businesses that are growing. They are a good source of passive income because you get to play no active role and share the profit. However, there are certain limitations on who can invest.

8.Build a Financial Planning, Investment and Insurance Business

This part actually applies to those that sell insurance. You receive an initial commission of your first sale, but that's not a passive income. The passive income occurs when you continue to receive renewal income for a policy you sold a long time ago. That's if you keep the client happy and on the book.

"A big part of financial freedom is having your heart and mind free from worry about the what-ifs of life."

Suze Orman

Bottom Line: The most important element you need on your journey towards financial freedom is, "patience" and "perseverance." It'll get tough, especially at the beginning. You might even decide to give up at some point. However, if you stick with the charted course, financial freedom would be your ultimate reward.

CHAPTER 13

TRAIT #4: CONTRIBUTING TO SOCIETY

Andy wanted to live a meaningful life, that was all he ever dreamed of. There was only one problem: he didn't understand what it meant to live a meaningful life. The term was subjective, and everybody has different views of what a meaningful life should be. So, he decided to pursue his own version of what a meaningful life should be, respect. If people respect you, then you must be doing something meaningful, he thought.

Andy started by pursuing knowledge, perhaps his existence would be meaningful if he was always the smartest man in the room, he told himself. He became a straight A student right from high school and finished top of his class at Harvard. Andy was always the smartest man in the room. However, a few weeks from his graduation, he came to another conclusion regarding the meaning of life, money.

Andy discovered that a larger percentage of his colleagues went to college because they hoped to earn a better income than those that didn't. The pursuit of financial freedom began at birth, he concluded. Andy decided that that living a meaningful life meant attaining financial freedom. He started spending less and investing more. The knowledge he had acquired over the years proved useful in charting a course towards his financial freedom. By the age of thirty, Andy was making an average of five hundred thousand dollars every year, and he was already a millionaire. Yet, the meaning of his existence still eluded him.

At 40, Andy had a secured future. He had the financial freedom he craved, but no future to live for. He had kidney disease and was dying without understanding the meaning of his life. He never got married, and had no offspring. He had resigned to die a lonely man.

That night, the hospital called him, his doctor wanted him to come in for a kidney transplant. He was getting another kidney, another chance at life. Andy could not believe his luck, and he certainly could not understand how a stranger could give him something so valuable. He finally concluded what it meant to live a meaningful life.

After his recovery, Andy set up a charity foundation to help people with kidney disease, and contributed 95% of his annual income. He volunteered at homeless shelters and started teaching at the community college. He wanted to contribute as much as he could to society because he had finally understood. A person cannot have a meaningful life without contributing.

Invested Millennials that are on their way to attaining (or have attained) financial freedom usually turn their energy toward philanthropy. They contribute to society as a way of giving back to a community that has given them so much, and as a way of making the world a better place. There are three ways Invested Millennials contribute to society.

1. Selfless givebacks (Focus to give, not monetary gains)
2. Impacting others' lives
3. Leaving a legacy they're proud of to society.

SELFLESS GIVEBACKS

Invested Millennials give back to their communities through charitable contributions. They sometimes set up investments for the sole purpose of using the profit to fulfill their charitable goals. Others work with the non-profit organization, donating their time, and providing invaluable advice.

As much as we don't like to talk about it, deep down inside, we are aware that there are some people living below the breadline and eking out their days in great poverty. In case you need a little nudge in the right direction, here are some importance of giving back to society.

IMPORTANCE OF GIVING BACK

1. A Feeling of Gratitude

When we give to people less fortunate than ourselves, we get a feeling of compassion, humanity, and a sense of appreciation. It allows us to view the world from another point of viewand gives us an understanding of how much we should be grateful for.

2. Become a Better Person

Engaging in charitable acts increases your emotional awareness, how much you care, and your consideration for others. This makes you in touch with your humanity and helps you grow as a human.

3. Alleviate Poverty

Whether we donate to a cause, volunteer our time, or get involved in corporate giving, selfless acts can help provide instant relief from poverty. An act of charity can help put food in someone's mouth, clothe another person, or provide access to basic sanitation.

4.Provides People with a Foundation for Future Development

In December 2012, Mark Zuckerberg and his wife Priscilla Chan announced that over the course of their life, they would give most their wealth to "advancing human potential and promoting equality." When you give back to society by investing in the potential of others, you are essentially providing the building blocks necessary for their future development. Accordingly, the development of society.

5. A Culture of Giving

A lot of people who give back to society were inspired by someone around them who had done the same. This means that, when you give, you inexplicably created a need to give in another person. It would start with the idea that would eventually manifest as a behavior, and we all know that behavior is contagious.

6.It Makes Us Feel Good

When you give to society, there is a significant increase in subjective well-being, accompanied by a boost in morale, and a sense of purpose. The sense of purpose comes from knowing that you have made a difference in someone else's life.

Regardless of how we choose to view it, giving back to society is not only beneficial to the recipients, but also to you, the giver.

You don't have to have to make a lot of money to donate, the smallest effort on your part makes a lot of difference to a person in need. Now that you know how important it is to give back to society, here are some ways you can give back as an Invested Millennial.

1. Provision of Food and Shelter

Start by devoting your time to the homeless. You can volunteer at soup kitchens and shelters. Donate resources such as clothing, blankets, toiletries, and non-perishable food.

2. Don't forget the children

There are many ways children can benefit from your giving back. Find a community center in your area that has a program for kids, and get involved. It won't cost much to make a significant impact in a child's life.

3. Use Your Skill to Teach and Help

You can use your skill to teach and help those in need. If you are good at playing or teaching music, then create a music program for a school that doesn't have one. You can start by getting people to donate secondhand musical instruments to teach the kids with. If you are a chef, cook food for elderly people. If you know how to knit, make baby clothes for your neighbor.

It doesn't matter what your skill is, there's always someone out there that'll need your service.

IMPACT OTHER LIVES

What does it mean to impact other lives?

In the most basic way, it refers to how you have made a person's life better by being part of it. Impacting other lives is often a consequence of giving back to society; however, it's on a more personal level. Jackie Robinson once said, "A life is not important except in the impact it has on other lives."It is the most important thing you can do as a human, to help other people live better, and help them achieve more than they thought possible.

When you make a habit of impacting people's lives, the ripple effect can last forever. You can help someone, who in turn helps someone else, that someone else could help another person, and the chain reaction would continue. This implies that how you touch a single life can have an impact on humanity as a whole.

You don't have to be rich to have an impact on another person's life, you don't even have to spend a penny. It starts with the simple things you do on a regular basis. Whether it's a word of encouragement to family or a friend, or a kind word and a smile to a stranger on the street, you are already impacting people's life without even knowing it.

If after introspection you discover that you don't do all that much, do not fret, start today. Begin by changing how you think, consider what you would have to believe in order to want to help others more. You need to find some type of motivation that will drive you towards this goal. Next, grab a piece of paper and make a list of things you can do to touch the lives of your friends and family. Act on the things you wrote down on a daily basis until it becomes a habit.

Begin slowly. Every week, pick one person whose life you intend to have a positive impact on. If you do that every week for a whole year, you would have touched at least 50 people's personal life. If those 50 each help 25 people, that's 1,250 lives in one year. Now imagine how many people you can help in a whole lifetime.

Impacting other lives should be a regular habit, do not wait until you have attained that financial freedom, or till you have a little money. This goes beyond giving back to society, it begins with the individuals around you. Motivate yourself until you start doing it, do it till you start loving it, and every night before you go to sleep, ask yourself how many lives you had touched that day. The answer will surprise you.

Leaving A Legacy They're Proud Of

We all want to be remembered for something we have achieved or contributed to the world. It can be the driving force that pushes us to accomplish extraordinary things, the desire to leave a legacy. What does the word "legacy" mean?

A legacy is something that is handed down from one to another, what we remember about a person long after they are gone. It's a way of saying "I was here, I contributed this, my life mattered."

There are different ways of leaving a legacy. The obvious one being, willing an inheritance to your survivors. While this is a decent thing to do, leaving a legacy that you can be proud of goes beyond material things. Another popular way of leaving a legacy is through our relationship with our loved ones. Even being a good role model is nice, we are talking about a more proactive approach towards leaving a legacy, consciously deciding to.

You could create a charity foundation or trust and endowing a scholarship to future students of any college of your choice. You could work with the college to arrange some type of annuity in which the school is chosen as the beneficiary when you die.

However, they have to pay you interest for as long as you are alive. Leaving a legacy is how you will be remembered; you need to be in control of that.

"Everyone must leave something behind when he dies . . . Something your hand touched some way so your soul has somewhere to go when you die . . . It doesn't matter what you do, so long as you change something from the way it was before you touched it into something that's like you after you take your hands away."

Ray Bradbury

Bottom Line: Your contribution to society through selflessly give back and impacting other's lives is the most important trait of an Invested Millennial. This allows you leaving a legacy you can be proud of. Remember; I was here, I contributed this, my life matters.

CHAPTER 14

THE TRANSFORMATION BEGINS WITH A MINDSET SHIFT

Changing our mindset, our core inner beliefs upon which we base our view of ourselves and the world is quite difficult. We all have a range of self-supporting beliefs that are based on negative conditioning, however, with the right tool, this mindset can be changed.

1.Mindset of Self-Confidence

The first mindset you need to acquire to make that transition from a poor procrastinator to an Invested Millennial is a belief in your capabilities. You need to convince yourself that you have what it takes to become financially free, by expelling any feeling of worthlessness often associated with low self-esteem.

This is why the first thing you have to do is to empower yourself with confidence and have the belief that you will be able to implement what you have learned in this book.

2.Mindset of Determination and Perseverance

After you have fashioned yourself into believing that you have the capacity to implement the things you learned in this book, the next step is for you to grow the determination and perseverance to see it through.

On your journey towards becoming an Invested Millennial, you'll fail to achieve some goals. Nevertheless, your reaction to this failure is what separates you from a poor procrastinator. When you have the determination and perseverance to push harder, you'll probably discover an alternate way of achieving your goal, and turn your failure into an opportunity to learn. Remember, true failure only comes when we stop trying.

3.Mindset of Taking Actions

Finally, you need to have a "take charge" mindset. Take a proactive approach towards your finance, especially when you are unsure because of lack of knowledge. A proactive mindset will push you to do the necessary research and acquire the skill to push your financial life in the right direction.

You can start your transition today by rearranging your belief system. Perform a mental exercise every night for 10 minutes.

Vividly picture yourself as an Invested Millennial. Before long, you'll start taking small actions to reinforce your new mindset.

"If my mind can conceive it, and my heart can believe it, I know I can achieve it."

Jesse Jackson

CHAPTER 15

PUT YOURSELT IN A PROPER ENVIRONMENT

You have developed the right mindset necessary to become an Invested Millennial, now you need to put yourself in the proper environment that inspires what you aim to achieve. The proper environment does not really exist; you have to create it yourself. Start by;

Finding People Who Dream Big Dreams and Take Great Actions.

You have to start hanging out with people that'll inspire you to want to be better, to become better. At some point in your journey, your motivation will wane when you encounter a minor setback. You would want to give up and let it all go. However, having people around you that dream big, and take great actions can serve as a source of inspiration.

Consequently, there are four sets of people you should avoid at all cost. Stay away from;

1. People that act in a negative manner.

2. People that appear pessimistic

3. People that make bad choices in life

4. People that are not motivated or driven towards their goal

Having the wrong set of people in your life can be truly detrimental to your success and well being. It's like trying to swim with bricks tied around your ankle, they'll always pull you down. It doesn't matter if you are a well-rounded, enlightened, hardworking, goal-oriented individual, if you surround yourself with the wrong people, they will bring you down in some way. They will end up stalling you from attaining your goals. Untie the bricks around your ankle, release yourself from the bondage, and watch yourself float towards financial freedom.

YOU ARE THE AVERAGE OF THE FIVE PEOPLE YOU ASSOCIATE WITH MOST

Having the right people in your life begins with the friends you choose to associate with. When it comes to making friends, as the saying goes, you are the average of the five people you associate with. The type of person you bring into your circle can touch your life positively or negatively if you are not careful.

The thing is, the friends you surround yourself with play a role in how you feel on a daily basis, and as a result, how you act. It all leads eventually to what you'll accomplish.

When it comes to having friends, you must be selective, you should pick your close friends wisely. Don't get me wrong, you can have as many acquaintances as you want, people you can talk to in a social setting. On the other hand, as far as your personal life is concerned, you should only surround yourself with like-minded individuals who are enlightened and will bring you up in life. As such, there are 3 types of people you must never associate with.

1. Stay away from a jealous friend. They secretly want you to fail.

2. Stay away from friends that are lazy. They have no vision.

3. Basically, stay away from a poor procrastinator. They will pull you down.

The type of friends that will aid you in your transition from being a poor procrastinator, into an Invested Millennial:

1. Want you to succeed in life.

2. Have your best interest at heart.

3.   Are goal oriented and have an idea what they want to do in life.

4.   Know and understand that sometimes you have to put yourself first.

5.   Are striving towards their own dream.

6.   Are motivated and diligent when it comes to priorities.

Remember, it is better to be alone than to be in a relationship with the wrong person.

BE THE STUPIDEST PERSON IN THE ROOM. DON'T BE THE SMARTEST PERSON IN THE ROOM

Now, don't get me wrong, I'm not telling you to be stupid, just the stupidest one in the room. What this means is that you should always surround yourself with people smarter than you. Why should you do this? Relax, I'll tell you.

After you have achieved a little financial knowledge, and the success that goes with it, you might consider yourself an expert on the topic, and close your mind to learning new things. You might even start getting cocky, and begin to focus on solutions, rather than sitting with the problem to understand its nature. This can lead to overconfidence.

To learn from the smartest people, there are a couple of things you need to be willing to change:

1. No more business as usual, you need to be willing to try new ways of doing things.
2. You need to stop staying quiet for fear of being the dumbest person in the room.
3. You need to be willing to give up your status as an expert. Recognize your shortcomings and what you need help with
4. You need to understand that people that can actually help you are smarter than you, at least in their domain.

Average Millennials are generally narcissistic in nature; they are crazy in love with themselves. This makes them want to answer every question and make every decision on their own. This can lead to a lot of costly mistakes. As much as I understand the importance of learning from mistakes, it is far better to (and easier) to surround yourself with smart people, leveraging their mistakes, and learning from it.

An Invested Millennial teams up with smart people who can provide direct answers relevant to their field of expertise.

Take a look at the people around you, are they the smartest people in the room? Here are things to look out for in smart people you should team up with.

1. They'll always surprise you with their new ideas and creative approach to problem-solving.
2. They convince with actions and question rather than dictate solutions.
3. They always have the big picture in sight.
4. They are active listeners, who never speak defensively
5. They are open-minded and willing to learn from you
6. You learn a lot from them.

One of the fastest ways of becoming an Invested Millennial is by surrounding yourself with people that are smarter than you. Don't let your ego get in the way of your success, don't let it get in the way of your financial freedom. Be humble.

"If you choose bad companions, no one will believe that you are anything but bad yourself."

Aesop

Bottom Line: Putting yourself in a proper environment basically means surrounding yourself with people that are smarter than you, people that can push you towards what you truly seek; financial freedom.

Chapter 16

Start Producing, Stop Consuming

You spent hours every day reading about the disadvantages of financial procrastination, and you have read a lot about how to be proactive. You have studied everything you need to become an invested Millennial but haven't started the work. I'll start later, you told yourself. You are a consumer, not a producer. It's time to stop your mindless consumption of information, and start producing.

What does it mean to be a producer?

When you begin your day as a producer, it means consuming information with the purpose of acting on it, and you do. Basically, a producer produces a result.

In contrast, as a consumer, you spend hours researching a topic you don't intend to act on. Sometimes the information consumed might not even be relevant to your goals in life. Example of such is, reading other people's Facebook status.

Analyzing what you are supposed to be doing doesn't count as producing. It's just a lie you tell yourself that you are productive, in reality, you are just –well, analyzing. You would take in so much information, but none will help you get closer to your goals. This is a way of procrastinating, it is a way of putting off what you need to do, what you know you are meant to be doing.

These are 5 steps to help you start producing, and stop consuming.

1. Things Don't Have to Be Perfect

You are consuming so much information to prepare yourself for the time you'll ultimately start working on your goal. You are waiting for the right time, maybe you want to complete your financial education before opening a savings account. I have two words for you; start producing.

Now is the best time to start working on your goals. You can spend your whole life waiting for that perfect time to open a savings account, the time will never arrive. Do you know why? It's because the perfect time doesn't exist. Shocking? Yes, I know, but it's the truth.

You know what exists, your financial responsibilities, your family, and a possible future of penury. All these things increase every day you postpone producing. So start by doing simple tasks every morning that gets you close to your goal.

2.Set a Deadline

Create a sense of urgency by setting a deadline of producing information consumed. There are two things you'll achieve by setting this deadline. It prevents you from consuming information you can't produce and pushes you to get things done.

For example, after reading this book, you can set a task of automating your accounts. The task should be simple enough to achieve, and the deadline should be close to creating a set of urgency.

3.Take a Step Every Day

You spend an hour after waking up on your bed, reading Facebook updates, and another on Twitter, consuming things you don't really need. Dedicate those productive hours of the morning producing. You want to write a book, write it. if you want to lose weight, lose it. Just do it within the two hours you spent reading social media updates. Do it every day until it becomes a habit.

4.Stop Over thinking

Consuming too much information can be so overwhelming to the senses, you soon find yourself thinking of all the problems that are likely to pop up ahead. So, rather than encountering the problems, you do nothing.

Stop over thinking, and stop over planning, just do it. Eventually, when the problems come, trust me, you will be able to deal with them.

"The way to get started is to quit talking and begin doing."

Walt Disney

Bottom Line: Your transformation from a poor procrastinator to an invested Millennial begins with a change in mindset. Change your mindset of mindless consuming, and start producing. After a successful shift in mindset, you need to put yourself in the right environment to help attain this goal.

CHAPTER 17

YOU WILL BE REWARDED IF YOU ARE PERSISTENT

The bell rang, it was the seventh round. Johnny stepped back into the ring, gloves held high to protect his already swollen face, as he danced in circles. With one eye knocked shot, his vision was already blurry. But he wasn't going to give up, he wasn't going to lose the fight on a technicality, he had something to prove.

Johnny was a 45-year-old boxer who had never won a fight since he began his career. He always got knocked down, and never got back up, he never saw a reason to. Well, that was about to change. Johnny had been knocked down three times that night, and each time, he got back up.

The twenty-something-year-old opponent threw another left hook, which hit him squarely in the jaw. But he held his ground, he didn't drop. Instead, he leaned on the red rope behind him, and fought off a rain of punches. As Johnny deflected each punch, he let his mind wander a little.

Twenty-four months before that night, he had torn his ligament in an accident. Everyone told him to quit. He was old and had never won a fight, they had said. Johnny did just the opposite. Every day, he worked harder, pushed himself to his limit, and got better.

Johnny was a forty-five-year-old man trying to make a comeback, everyone expected him to fail. Everyone, except his four years old son. So, every time he got knocked down that night, he simply thought of the little boy watching and got back up.

So far, Johnny had lasted seven rounds. The twenty-something-year-old opponent was tired, it was obvious. His punches were weaker, and not as direct as the previous rounds. Johnny decided to take a risk, he extended his right fist and landed two consecutive sucker punch. He then finished with a left hook. The opponent dropped, Johnny tore his ligament again, and the crowd went wild.

Through the whole commotion, Johnny only thought of his son, he imagined the little boy smiling at him from beyond the grave. Indeed, he had something to prove. The twenty-something years old opponent stayed down.

What does it mean to be persistent?

The moral of the story is simple; you only truly fail when you stop trying. This is the fundamental difference between a poor procrastinator and an Invested Millennial.

In your journey towards financial freedom, you will encounter the most difficult situation. You'll probably lose thousands of dollars. At that point, your goal might appear impossible to achieve, fight that thought, and persevere. It's quite simple, when you are scared, persevere, when you encounter obstacles, persevere, and when everyone tells you to quit, persevere.

Here are a couple of steps that can help you develop perseverance

- Decide what your purpose is, and set goals that will help you achieve this purpose
- Prepare yourself for obstacles and setbacks, remember do not over think.
- Take the first step needed to attain your goals.
- If things don't go as expected, reevaluate the whole process, devise a new plan and start again

- Garner support and encouragement, stay away from naysayers
- Maintain focus, never doubt yourself
- Enjoy your accomplishment

"A river cuts through rock, not because of its power, but because of its persistence."

Jim Watkins

Bottom Line: At some point in your life, you were a poor procrastinator, then you took the first step towards becoming an Invested Millennial by deciding to finish this book. But it's not enough for you to consume, you have to produce.

You are about to embark on a lifetime journey filled wilt obstacles, and major setbacks. It will get tough, your motivation will wane, you'll experience fear, and you'll fail. However, you'll get back up and keep fighting, because you understand that even though you failed at different points on your journey, you are not a failure. Perseverance is your salvation; persistence will see you through.

Chapter 18

Your Journey From Poor Procrastinator to Invested Millennial

We have finally gotten to the last part of the book, and here you are still. You could have dropped the book for a Netflix series, but you didn't. You completely understand who a poor procrastinator is, and already have an in-depth understanding of the traits of an Invested Millennial.

Now, here's the part where you need to figure out,
A question...

How would you envision yourself 5 years from now?

I can't answer this question for you and certainly don't expect you to be able to answer it either, at least not yet. However, the answer to this question can help you significantly increase your productivity as an invested Millennial.

BONUS

ADDITIONAL RESOURCES FOR YOU

AN IGNORANT PROCRASTINATOR

This is a self-evaluation worksheet to help you to determine how much it would cost you in dollars if you delayed in your financial journey.

Get your worksheet in the following link:

https://theinvestedmillennial.com/wp-content/uploads/2017/12/How-Much-Is-It-Costing-You.xlsx

So, have you download the worksheet? Here's how you can use the spreadsheet.

1. Enter your birth date (In the format of MM/DD/YYYY)
2. Set and write down the investment target for yourself, i.e. how much investment contribution monthly can you commit? For how many years? And what's the annual rate of return you are looking for? Lastly, what's the holding period of the investment (This is important for it would help you to have a clear understanding on what kind of investment vehicles you should look for.)

3. In the 'INVEST NOW' column, Key-in your target into the spreadsheet, the first and the end date of your investment contribution, your monthly contribution, and the rate of return you are looking for.

4. Similarly, in the 'INVEST LATER' column, assume if you invest at a later stage of your age, say 5 years or 10 years from now. Enter those dates, and try to match the same contribution, annual rate of return and the investing period from the 'INVEST NOW' column.

5. Here's the fun part where the role of time and interest came into play. Key in the selling date of your investment, make sure the dates in both columns are the same for easy comparison. (Ideally, you should hold your investment for a minimum of 5 years, the longer the better)

6. As the worksheet calculated automatically for you, you will see how much is it costing you literally. The numbers might be shocking to you, hence the reason you should start investing today!

7. You can experiment around with the worksheet, keying different values

A CLEAR PICTURE OF YOUR DEBT

You have heard of words to prioritize your debt, to pay off the lowest debt balance, to repay your high-interest debt balance, and so on. But those words never answer your one simple question. Which is How?

The methodology is very simple, start being proactive in your finance, by planning ahead, first list down all the loans/mortgages you owned. This include every outstanding amount, the interest rates.

To help you to have a clear picture, a powerful worksheet was created for you, called 'DEBT REPAYMENT CHEATSHEET', now download from the link below.

https://theinvestedmillennial.com/wp-content/uploads/2017/12/Debt-Clearing-Cheatsheet.xlsx

CREDIT CARD BILLS

1. List down all your credit cards, loans, mortgages, with the outstanding amount, the rates incurred, and the minimum repayment monthly for each debt.

2. Prioritize on the smaller and high-interest bill, (i.e. credit card bill with an 18% APR where you can payoff within 3 months)

3. Find out how much you afford to pay more for your debts. i.e. you have allocated total $1k monthly for repayments of all your debts, find out if you can increase by additional S100 or $200 monthly, this could be achieved by cutting unnecessary expenses or monthly subscription.

4. While maintaining the minimum repayment for the rest of your debts, and using the cheat-sheet, find out the time you can cut off the debt and how much you can save from interest by paying more to the high-interest bill.

5. Set-up a reminder of repayment schedule for this highest-interest bill, this will help you to avoid late payment of bill which incurred additional penalty.

6. Next, following the same steps, redistribute your monthly allocated repayment amount to other bills

LOAN REPAYMENT

1. To help on your loan repayment, additional research is required. You must understand the 2 types of personal loans plan available:

a. Balance Transfer (providing interest free periods of 3 months to 1 year, a one-time fee will be charged)

b. Debt Consolidation (installment loan that lends you a lump sum which adhere to a lower fixed rate)

2. The general rule of the thumb is: If you make enough money to repay your balance within 12 months, go for a balance transfer option; If you need more than 1 year to pay off your loan in full, go for a debt consolidation option.

3. Research the plans available in the market, by using the cheat-sheet in loan repayment, find out the suitable loan-terms, monthly repayment, while considering the total interest payable.

FINDING YOUR FINANCIAL INDEPENDENT NUMBER (FIN)

How much money do you need to be financial freedom? Is it one million? Is it two million?

This is a big misconception on financial freedom, truth is you don't need a lot of money to achieve financial freedom. it is not the amount of money which you should accumulate, focus should be on the freedom of time itself.

First understanding your monthly expenses and special requirements, as you'd want to cover everything. These include,

- Rent
- Utilities
- Transportation
- Bills
- Groceries
- Eating out
- Shopping
- Entertainment
- Subscriptions

While some values would fluctuate from month to month, just take the average. Your FIN number is the sum of all the expenses. Knowing this figure will help you how or when you would become financially free.

As explained earlier, financial freedom is not a certain amount of money sitting in your bank account. It is when your passive income exceeds your FIN number.

How would your passive income cover this number? As a Millennial, focus on this:

-    Investment
-    Royalties

Your Investing Roadmap

When it comes to investing, go for KISS principle, Keep it simple, stupid.

The answer is the dollar-cost averaging (DCA) in Index fund ETF.

It is a no-brainer strategy that will work best for Millennials, who have no time to monitor their investment. Just set up an automatic investing account and make the transfer from your savings account to the fund monthly, and you need not worry whether the market is going up or down. Why? Because you will get more units as the market goes down and purchase fewer units as it goes up. In the end, they will just average.

The principle requires you to invest for a minimum period of duration (5 – 10 years), and the investment will come in two types of gains,

- Capital gain where the investment increase in value
- Dividend gain are distributions by a company to its stockholders (Your passive income source)

Meanwhile, depending on the country you reside in, taxation will be different for ETF capital gain and dividend. For instance, in Singapore, a one-tier corporate tax system is adopted, where all dividends paid by a company are exempt from tax in the hands of the shareholders.

A worksheet to help you determine how much you should invest and how much dividend you will get from the investment.

Get your worksheet in the following link:

https://theinvestedmillennial.com/wp-content/uploads/2017/12/Passive-Dividend-Generator.xlsx

To use the spreadsheet:

STEPS

1.   Research the ETF funds, making sure that they are low-cost, index-based and diversified.

2.   Find out the annual capital gain and dividend yield of the investment.

3.   Determine your annual investment amount and investment period.

4.   The estimated dividend payout will be calculated for you.

UNDERSTANDING RETURN ON INVESTMENT

Return on investment can be defined as the benefit to an investor resulting from an investment of some resource. Consequently, a high return on investment implies that the gains compare favorably with the cost and vice versa.

Return on investment in the business is used to evaluate the performance and the efficiency of an investment, or to compare the performance and efficiency of other investments. It can be calculated by dividing the benefit (or return) of investment by the cost of investment. The result is then expressed in percentage or ratio.

The major advantage of expressing the result in percentage is that; it allows you measure different types of investment against each other. You will find it easier to compare the variety of investments within your portfolio, to decide which is most profitable.

Increase Your Return on Investment

Your ability to increase your return on investment depends primarily on your skill at managing your investment options. You cannot use the same strategy for different investment options and hope it'll work. You cannot get lucky; it takes deliberate planning. Essentially, you need to know how to handle your finances.

These are easy ways of increasing your return on investment for different investment choices:

Max Out Your Retirement Accounts

A smart investment plan begins with a vision of your long-term financial goal, and nothing screams "long-term" like your retirement account. Therefore, the first thing to do is to check the limit set by the government on annual contribution. Next, increase your contribution percentage every year.

The maximum you can invest in both your 401(k) and workplace retirement account per year is $16,500. However, if you are 50 years old, or above, your maximum increases to $22,000. Your IRAs /Roth IRAs have a limit of $5,000, which increases to $6,000 if you are over 50 years' old.

Don't Forget Your Savings Account

By now, you already know what automation is and how you can use it to boost your finance. You should make it a goal to automate the transfer of at least 20% of your annual income from your checking account to your savings account, certificate of deposit account, or taxable brokerage account.

Distribute Your Assets Wisely

Don't just put all your money into your retirement and savings account, distribute the money equally. You can start by spending 40% of your money on fixed-income investments such as real estate commodities, and bonds. This type of investment generates annual interest.

The remaining 60% should spread across cap stocks, index funds, mutual funds, foreign stocks, money market, and precious metals. Diversification is the key here.

Control the Cost

The cost of your investments matter. Every dollar you pay as account fees from finance advisers, commission for ETF trades, commissions for stocks, expense ratios on your mutual funds, and taxes, is a dollar less of potential return. What do you do? Keep your expenses lower than 1% of your finance portfolio. The more you pay for advice and finance management, the less your return of investment.

Rebalance Your Finance Portfolio Annually

After you have filled your portfolio with investments that interest you, the next step is to maintain the time, money, and effort dedicated to each investment to keep it balanced. Different investments generate different returns over time. Accordingly, your portfolio can drift from its target allocation, which creates a different risk-return characteristic you can't account for.

The major purpose of a balancing strategy is to maintain targeted risks.

Manage Your Taxes Well

The highest expense you'll probably incur in a portfolio is your taxes. There are three categories of tax management that you'll need as an investor. They are;

• Asset allocation: In which you spread your investment across different accounts based on tax efficiency. It essentially involves sending of the most tax-efficient investments into taxable accounts and the least tax-efficient investments into non-taxable or tax-deferred account.

- Withdrawal order: Retirees will find this method of tax management most useful. It is the smart withdrawal of your money from a retirement account without incurring too much money in taxes. It comes from understanding the consequences of withdrawal of assets from different retirement accounts.

- Tax-Loss harvesting: This is a way of making your investment portfolio work harder for you by generating potential tax savings. You can do this by selling investments that have declined in value at a loss, which would subsequently generate a tax deduction and lower your taxes. The tax-loss can then be used to offset your future gains.

- Be Disciplined: Finally, all the best investment strategy in the world is useless if you lack the discipline to see it through. In order to maintain a long-term perspective of your financial goals, a disciplined approach towards investment is required.

WHAT IS THE VALUE OF YOUR TIME?

How people value time varies depending on the kind of work they do, the part of the world they live, how much they earn, and how much they expect to earn in the future.

Why should you know the worth of your time? Now, this is one question I can answer for you. There are many resources that'll be utilized on your journey towards financial freedom, one of them is your time. Time is a finite resource; whose use or misuse determines your success or failure in life.

Knowing exactly how much your time is worth can help you decide how to prioritize your tasks. For example, if you had the option of writing an article, or speaking at a seminar for a fee, which would you pick? The answer to that question depends on the number of hours it will take and the value of your time in dollars.

It also helps you decide which task to manage yourself, and which to outsource. Now, imagine that your time is worth $50 per hour, and you spent twelve hours doing your taxes, that's $600. Bearing in mind, that you could have easily hired an accountant to do the same task for $500, was your time well spent?

Before I continue, let me be the first to state that, not everything in life has a monetary value. Time spent with your loved ones is priceless, cherish it. You can't simply skip your kid's piano recital because it isn't worth your time in dollars. That said, here is how to calculate exactly how much your time is worth. Grab a calculator, and let's begin.

STEPS

Step One

Start by calculating how much money you make within a particular period after filing your taxes. The period you pick has to be relevant to what you do. Which means, if you are a monthly salary earner, the monthly figure makes sense.

If you are a business owner, an annual figure (which include your salary, compensation, and your share of the company's profit) is the way to go. For example, if you own 25% of a company that makes an average of $100,000 annually, the figure you'll use is $25,000 + your basic salary.

If your figure is in a flux, no problem. Just take the average over a long period of time. For the purpose of this calculation, we'll say you earn $100,000 per year. Are you there? Good, now let's go to the next step.

Step Two

Next, calculate how many hours you spent working within that period. The hours spent working must include time spent in the office, time spent traveling, answering emails and phone calls, etc.

If you don't have an accurate figure, I suggest you track your time for two weeks using either an online time tracker or a paper planner. We need to have a clear picture of your working hours before we can continue. For the purpose of this example, we'll use 2,000 hours a year.

Step Three

This is the part you'll need a calculator for. Simply divide your total net earnings by the number of hours worked. Mathematically that can be expressed as;

Value of Time = Total Net Earnings ÷ Number of Hours Worked

Using the example above, that is

Value of Time = 100,000 ÷ 2,000

Value of Time = $50 per hour.

This implies that, if you work 2,000 hours for an annual salary of $100,000, the value of your time is $50/ hour. You get the idea, don't you?

After you have calculated the value of your time, the next thing is to apply the result in different scenarios in your life to maximize your time. Here is how;

Write a complete hourly breakdown of your daily activities, from mowing the lawn to your administrative tasks. Next, find out the cost of outsourcing, and make the comparison. The investment is good if you find someone that'll do your tasks for less than your own time is worth.

For example, you spent 5 hours on a DIY website, designing a new business card. Still going with the assumption of $50/hour, that's $250 worth of time. On the other hand, you could have easily hired a person for less than $250 to do the same task.

You can also apply this criterion to evaluate opportunities. Calculate how much you'll make, and how much time you would have to invest, if the figure doesn't add up, it isn't worth it.

Don't forget, you can't always judge the value of time spent based on the financial worth. Time spent doing tasks that truly makes you happy, moments spent with your family, and hours donated to a good cause are priceless, cherish them.

Once you understand the concept of economic value of time, you can start making a lot of wiser decisions in life. We must realize that at any given time, if we choose to do one thing, we have to give up the opportunity of another thing.

If there is a lunch promotion at a restaurant and you can save 10 bucks, would you queue for half an hour just to get in when your economic value of time is $50/hour?

The point is your time is priceless. Stop wasting it. Use it wisely to create another opportunity.

Your time is limited, so don't waste it living someone else's life. Don't be trapped by dogma - which is living with the results of other people's thinking. Don't let the noise of others' opinions drown out your own inner voice. And most important, have the courage to follow your heart and intuition.

Steve Jobs

BRAINSTORMING YOUR POTENTIAL SOURCE OF PASSIVE INCOME

Now knowing your FIN number, and better understanding of your income. The following session will help you to find your next source of income.

Please spent 30 -60min of your time for the following.

Main Job_____

Hourly Rate_____

What is your Potential Source of Income (It could be related to your job, or the skills you have)

Sub-category is how you could monetize them (It could be based on your hourly rate)

1. _____

a. _____

b. _____

2. _____

a. _____

b. _____

3. _____

   a. _____

   b. _____

4. _____

   a. _____

   b. _____

Here's some ideas for you to get started:

https://theinvestedmillennial.com/wp-content/uploads/2017/12/Passive-Income-Idea.xlsx

FINANCIAL FREEDOM IS PEACE OF MIND

You have better understanding on investment dividend, as well as passive income you could potentially create. The next is to answer the very first question you have earlier,

How would your passive income cover this number? As a Millennial, focus on this:

- Investment
- Royalties

It is just a simple math calculation.

Let's say your FIN number = $2500
Average dividend you have = $500

So your other passive income source should cover $2000 ($2500-$500) so you would be financially free.

Imagine you have an online-business, there are multiple ways you can be financially free.

By generating $2 per sale, you'd need 1000 sales monthly, or

By generating $250 per sale, you'd need 8 sales monthly

Sure, this would need a lot of front-loaded work. But wouldn't you rather struggle the first 5 years of your working life than the rest of your life working a 9-5?

CONCLUSION

Chapter 1: What is Financial procrastination

In this chapter, the why millennials tend to procrastinate financial issues Is explained. An in-depth study of the reasons is given and have been stated out. The major reasons being fear of unknown, difficulty in understanding and the millennial tendency of avoiding.

Chapter 2: Are You Being Reactive or Proactive in Finance

The necessity of being financially stable has been stated in this chapter. Managing money to save for future, the plan you must have for the future and saving money for when there is an emergency.

Chapter 3: The Cost of Financial Procrastination

There is a cost you'll be eventually paying if you avoid your financial issues right now Sloppy work, filling in your taxes late and other things that will cost you in the long run. These along with a simple illustration of daily commute fare and how it is costing you if you are sloppy has been explained.

Chapter 4: How Time Value of Money Affects You

The simple mathematics of long run that most people avoid looking into is explained on a personal and professional level. Illustrations of times where the money lies in future and you spending it now and buying things on credit. There are also examples to show how different marketing and other contracts affect or effect your business with time.

Chapter 5: How Much Does It Cost You

The increasing inflation leads to decrease in value of money. This chapter focuses on that aspect of money. Where big returns in the future are actually a fraction of the money you'll be investing in it now. This depleting value of money is explained with mathematical equations and examples.

Chapter 6: Automation is the Solution

Automation has been stated as the future of finance for all types of businesses. The ways automation has increased the efficiency of business and its accuracy has been stated. However, the bad aspect that is loss of jobs for a lot of people has also been shown.

Chapter 7: Now is The Time to Invest in Your Future

In this chapter, the need of investing has been demonstrated with a step-by-step guide to go about it. Starting early has been proved to be really beneficially, however, it has also been recommended to not to jump into investments. Learning and understanding investments, investing wisely and investing time to get good gains from investment is the key feature.

Chapter 8: Are You a Poor Procrastinator

There are various types of procrastinators and there are different solutions to each one of them. The solutions are stated out through the problem, however, there are some common traits as well. This chapter, focuses on the solutions you can use, or rather the life hacks you can use to change yourself from being a procrastinator and getting big in life.

Chapter 9: Who Are the Invested Millennials?

People who are called millennials and what makes them millennials has been said in this chapter. How an invested millennial is different from an average millennial, what makes them different and their traits have been shown. These traits are then further explained in the following chapters.

Chapter 10: Trait #1: Having Clear Goals in Life

Having a clear goal is the first trait of an invested millennial. Having a clear goal, having a belief in your goal, and the problems you'll face and how to go about them are the key features of being an invested millennial. Goals are shown to change your outlook towards life and you'll be able to change your life, if you know where you are headed.

Chapter 11: Trait #2 They Value in Themselves

The second trait shows how invested millennials value themselves and invest time in themselves. They invest their money very wisely and are not sloppy with their money matters. Seeking to invest money is not the only act, but investing time with money to get bigger gains in their returns is what makes an invested millennial.

Chapter 12: Trait #3 On the Way/ Have Attained Financial Freedom

Having financial freedom doesn't only mean having enough money to survive the day. The chapter shows how you can value everything against time and invest wisely. Dividing your salary on hourly basis, knowing your investment and returns well lets you have an idea of your money flow. The chapter also focuses on having multiple sources of income and a passive income.

Chapter 13: Trait #4: Making a Contribution to Society

Only focusing on yourself is important, however, making a contribution to the society is equally important. Unless, we make a difference in lives of people there is no way we would be able to leave a mark, a legacy of our own, for the world to remember.

Chapter 14: THE TRANSFORMATION BEGINS WITH A MINDSET SHIFT

The transformation is not easy, it needs you to get out of your chair and change your mindset, change your surrounding and get out of all the negativity around you.

Chapter 15: PUT YOURSELT IN A PROPER ENVIRONMENT

The chapter shares a mantra of "being stupidest in the room" and states that you are the average of 5 people around you.

Chapter 16: Start Producing, Stop Consuming

Being a producer is the best way to stop spending and start earning. But being a producer isn't going to be easy if you do not live by deadlines and stop overthinking and wasting time on the choices you've already made.

Chapter 17: "You Will be Rewarded If You Stay Persistence"

Staying persistent is what has seemed to pay off for a lot of people on this world. You are going to make something of yourself if and only if you don't stop and keep pushing towards your goals. It's going to be hard at start with no returns, but it will be worth it.

Chapter 18: Your Journey from Poor Procrastinator to Invested Millennial

The book ends with a self-evaluation sheet that anyone can use to make a change in their lives.

ACKNOWLEDGMENTS

I would like to first express my gratitude to the main entity that inspired me to write this book. Woei W, this book wouldn't exist if not your insight and perspectives.

Thank you, my mom and dad, for having trust in me, and your priceless advice and recommendations that made my book way better.

I particularly want to thank the following individuals for their input, as well as encouragement: Andrew, Jimmy, Hazel, Lionel, Alvin, Chris, Jay, Sean, Jason, Terry, YK, JY, TH, RH, I am forever grateful for your honest and kind feedback. Thanks for paving the way for me!

DISCLAIMER

This book and its contents are for general informational purposes only. It is not intended and as personal investment, tax, or legal advice, or recommendation. The book also should not be construed as an offer to sell or the solicitation of an offer to buy, nor as a recommendation to buy, hold, or sell any security.

The author is not a registered investment advisor, a registered securities broker dealer, or a certified financial planner, or otherwise licensed to give investment advice. The information and opinions provided in this book should not be relied upon or used as a substitute for consultation with professional advisors.

The use of or reliance on the contents of this book is done solely at your own risk. All opinions, analyses, and information included herein are based on sources believed to be reliable, and the book has been written in good faith, but no representation or warranty of any kind, expressed or implied, is made, including but not limited to any representation or warranty concerning accuracy, completeness, correctness, timeliness, or appropriateness.

In no event shall any reference to any third party or third-party product or service be construed as an approval or endorsement by the author. In particular, the author does not endorse or recommend the services of any particular broker, dealer, mutual fund company, or information provider.

ABOUT THE AUTHOR

JEREMY KHO is a millennial in his early 30s. He is a self-published author, an individual investor, an engineer, and an online marketer. He had 5 years of experience in the consultancy firm in Singapore, and that experiences he acquired had helped on his journey from being a poor procrastinator to becoming a financially free invested millennial.

He had started his financial journey and investing in his early 20s, where he had been applying the same strategy in this Book. He had learned the idea on finances and investing during his career path, and he had learned from the books and courses on money matters, that with the correct money mindset, along with the knowledge and tool, toward financial freedom and a rich life is entirely possible.

Additional details about Jeremy, and the materials he offers can be found at:

Website   :Stress Proof Your Money

Facebook   :www.facebook.com/stressproofyourmoney

Twitter   : twitter.com/SProofYourMoney

THANK YOU FOR READING MY BOOK

May I ask you a favor? If you got anything out of this book or if you have any comments. I appreciate all of your feedback and I love hearing what you have to say on the book.

Please leave me a helpful review on Amazon letting me know your thought. Your input will help make the next version of this book and my future books better.

Leave a review on this book's product page. (https://www.amazon.com/review/create-review?asin=B078PNS4TT)

Thank You!
~Jeremy Kho~

OTHER BOOKS BY JEREMY KHO

The Passive Aggressive Earner
(https://www.amazon.com/dp/B07B6QRNBX)

The Journey From Poor Procrastinator to Invested Millennial
(https://www.amazon.com/dp/B078PNS4TT)

The Millennial Roadmap to a Rich Life
(https://www.amazon.com/dp/B01LX2PMXD)

The Millennial Guide to Success in Stock Investing
(https://www.amazon.com/dp/B01N3XMG51)

The Millennial Guide to Success in Mutual Fund Investing
(https://www.amazon.com/dp/B01NBP1XG4)

Time Value of Money Decoded
(https://www.amazon.com/dp/B06XSNHHZL)

Being Rich? How Serious Are You?
(https://www.amazon.com/dp/B073PCQFHV/)

Made in the USA
San Bernardino, CA
03 December 2018